The Psychology Thes

Also by T.R. Smyth

THE PRINCIPLES OF WRITING IN PSYCHOLOGY

The Psychology Thesis

Research and Coursework

T.R. Smyth

First published 2008 by
PALGRAVE MACMILLAN
Houndmills, Basingstoke, Hampshire RG21 6XS and
175 Fifth Avenue, New York, N.Y. 10010
Companies and representatives throughout the world

PALGRAVE MACMILLAN is the global academic imprint of the Palgrave Macmillan division of St. Martin's Press, LLC and of Palgrave Macmillan Ltd. Macmillan® is a registered trademark in the United States, United Kingdom and other countries. Palgrave is a registered trademark in the European Union and other countries.

ISBN-13: 978–0–230–00842–7 paperback
ISBN-10: 0–230–00842–9 paperback

This book is printed on paper suitable for recycling and made from fully managed and sustained forest sources. Logging, pulping and manufacturing processes are expected to conform to the environmental regulations of the country of origin.

A catalogue record for this book is available from the British Library.

A catalog record for this book is available from the Library of Congress.

10   9   8   7   6   5   4   3   2   1
17   16   15   14   13   12   11   10   09   08

Printed in China

To Elizabeth and David

Contents

Acknowledgements   xi
A Note to Students   xii

1 Overview   **1**
   Variations   2
   Contribution   2
   Expectations   3
   The research   4
   Documenting the research   5
   Two-part research components   6
   Motivation   7

2 Time   **8**
   Time frame   9
   Deadlines   10
   Time management   10
   Planning time   10
   Target dates   12
   Estimating time   14
   Thinking   17
   Monitoring your work   18
   Some advice   18

3 Considerations   **20**
   Some general advice   20
   Individual vs group research projects   22
   Originality   24
   Quantitative vs qualitative research   25
   Theoretical basis   26
   Goals of scientific research   26
   Outcome   27
   Documenting the research   27
   Supervision   28
   Problems and advice   30
   The research   32

Other considerations 37
A closing note 38

4 Preparation **39**
Initial preparation 39
Research outline 45
Some advice 47

5 Detailed Design and Planning **48**
Research design and data analysis 49
Research involving multiple experiments
    or studies 61
Group research projects 61
Problems 65

6 Ethics **67**
Approval 67
Modifications 68
Considerations 68
Requirements 69
Children 72
Schools 72
Infants 72
Individuals who are unable to give informed consent 73
Special groups 73
Photographic or audio recording 73
Confidentiality 74
Deception 75
Dcbriefing 75
Survey research 76
Qualitative research 78
Potential problems 78
A comment 79

7 A Research Proposal **80**
Requirement 80
Time plan 80
Length 81
Content 81
Structure 81
Planning and writing a research proposal 83
Figures and tables 88
Drafts of research proposals 89

Pilot or validation research   89
Multiple experiments or studies   91
A word of advice   93

8   A Research Proposal Seminar   95
Anxiety   95
Content   96
Preparation   97
Confidence   100
Presentation   100
A final note   101

9   The Structure and Format of a Thesis   103
The basic structure   103
Format   108
Chapters of a thesis in book format   109
Structure of the parts   110

10   Writing a Thesis   111
Requirements of a thesis   111
Examination   112
Information and ideas   113
Ideas in a thesis   114
Parts of the thesis   115
Length of the parts   115
Planning   116
The introduction   118
The research   122
The discussion   125
Abstract   130
Back-up   131
Some advice on writing   132

11   Drafts and Editing   133
First working draft   133
Headings and pagination   134
Editing   134
Editing for content   135
A second opinion   139
Editing for consistency   139
Making changes   140
Editing for detail   140
Supervisors' drafts   142

Revising the first draft   147
The second supervisor's drafts   147
Some words of advice   148

12 Finalizing the Thesis   **149**
Editorial style   149
The body of the thesis   150
Report format   151
Figures and tables   153
Pagination   155
Reference list   156
Appendices   156
The composite file   157
Inserting pages   158
Proofreading   158
Preliminary pages   159
Spacing from top and bottom margins   162
Pagination   162
Final proofreading   162
Binding   162
Copies   163
The end   163

Appendices
A   Recommended style requirements for theses   164
B   An example of a title page   166
C   An example of a certificate page   167
D   An example of an acknowledgements page   168
E   An example of a table of contents page   169
F   An example of a list of figures page   170
G   An example of a list of tables page   171
H   An example of an abstract page   172

Notes   173
Index   175

Acknowledgements

This book owes its existence primarily to those who patiently supervised me – in particular Professor, T.J. Nettelbeck of the University of Adelaide – and to my colleagues over the years with whom I have discussed the subject matter. It also owes much to the students whose trials, tribulations, and successes motivated me to write it and to their experiences, which contributed to it. In addition, it owes much to Professor N. Bond (now at the University of Western Sydney), who encouraged me while I was at Flinders University to complete the writing of my first book (which in due course lead to the writing of this one), and who took the time to read and comment on an early draft of this book.

My thanks are due to the anonymous reviewers who took the time and effort to read and comment on the draft manuscript. Their comments were extremely helpful and contributed greatly to its content.

Last, but not least, I must acknowledge the staff of Palgrave Macmillan who contributed directly to the completion of this book. In particular, I owe a debt of gratitude to Mrs Anna van Boxel, who was patient with me through a trying period.

A Note to Students

Fulfilling the requirements of the research component of a programme of study that includes coursework helps you to extend your research knowledge and skills, and to develop a number of generic abilities that will stand you in good stead in the future. It also presents you with a challenge and the possibility of gaining rewards that are not so pragmatic.

Devising a piece of research gives you the opportunity to "walk on ground on which no one has walked before". Your research must involve some originality. Therefore, it provides you with the opportunity to add to the accumulated store of human knowledge. Although your addition will be relatively minor, this is equally true of the outcome of the vast majority of research. Therefore, you should derive some satisfaction from your modest contribution.

Reporting your research and its outcome in the form of a thesis gives you the opportunity to express your ideas in writing. In addition, because a copy of your thesis will be held in the university library indefinitely, it allows you to record your achievement in a lasting and publicly available form.

Of course, nothing that is worth achieving comes easily. The research component of a programme of study is no exception: It requires time and effort. On the other hand, if you plan your time, monitor your progress, and work steadily, you should be able to complete this component without particular difficulty.

You may initially approach the prospect of devising and carrying out a research project and writing a thesis with some trepidation, but you will already have the basic knowledge and skills required. Consequently, given the advice and guidance of your supervisor, and presuming that you are prepared to devote the necessary time and effort to the task ahead, you will successfully complete this component of your study and derive some satisfaction and a sense of achievement from doing so.

1 Overview

Honours, postgraduate diploma, masters,[1] and professional doctorate[2] programmes of study in psychology differ in duration and structure, but all include a substantial research component. The purpose of this is to give students the opportunity to develop their understanding of research and their ability to carry out an independent research project.

Devising and carrying out a piece of research and writing a thesis[3] makes students much more familiar with research. Moreover, doing so helps them to develop their analytical and critical thinking abilities. As a result, students who complete a research project and write a thesis are much better equipped to evaluate published research and to understand its implications and limitations. In addition, although many students will not become involved in basic research in their future careers, they may well become involved in applied research for some specific purpose – for example, in the form of evaluating a treatment programme. Developing their knowledge of research, therefore, is of value to students.

Another benefit of carrying out a research project is that it helps students to develop a number of generic skills and abilities that will be useful in their future careers. Planning and carrying out a research project is conceptually similar in many respects to planning and carrying out any project. The necessary tasks must be identified, planned in some sequence, and completed. In addition, the requirements of writing a thesis are similar to those involved in planning and writing any detailed and lengthy document, such as a proposal for some course of action, or the report of an investigation.

In any event, devising and carrying out a piece of research and interpreting and reporting the outcome are intellectually stimulating and rewarding. Commonly, students are excited by the opportunity to be creative, rather than simply studying research that others have carried out, and they find that they derive a feeling of satisfaction and the sense of achievement resulting from completion of their research projects and theses.

▶ Variations

There are variations in the contribution of the research component to a programme of study, the expected comprehensiveness and allowed length of the thesis, and the expected standard of work. Understanding how programmes of study can differ will help you to understand more clearly what is required of you in your specific programme. In addition, this understanding will help you to identify any questions that you might need to ask to clarify any uncertainties that you have about what is involved in the research component in the particular programme of study in which you are enrolled.

At a conceptual level, there is little difference between programmes in what is required in the research component. Put simply, it involves a student devising, carrying out, and documenting a research project under supervision. Usually, the research is documented in the form of a conventional thesis, but sometimes it is reported in the form of a journal article.[4]

This overview of the research component sets the context for the remainder of this book. It is, however, important to understand that while its contents – and that of the remainder of this book – are generally applicable, there will be instances in which there are some inconsistencies with the requirements of a given programme of study or policies of departments[5] and universities. When this is so, the requirements given to students for a particular programme and the policies of the department and university involved take precedence.

▶ Contribution

In a one-year honours programme that follows from a three-year undergraduate degree, and in the final year of a three- or four-year honours programme, the research component typically contributes between 30 and 50%. In a postgraduate diploma programme, the contribution is likely to be in the order of 30%.

Masters and professional doctorate programmes typically involve 2 years of study, and the contribution of the research component will vary with the structure of the programme. For example, the overall contribution of the research component might be 15%, but this could equate to 30% of the work in 1 year. It is also possible that students might be required to prepare their research projects and to submit a formal research proposal in the first year, and to carry out the research and write their theses in the second year. In this case, the contribution of the research component will be spread over 2 years.

▶ Expectations

What is expected in the research component varies with the programme of study and the policies of the department and university. It might also vary somewhat between individual supervisors, whose expectations can differ as a result of their past experiences, expectations, and preferences – but such differences can be expected to be minor. Typically, the following brief outlines are applicable.

Honours

Students at honours level are expected individually to identify a research problem that is of some importance, design and carry out one or more experiments or studies to investigate that problem, and submit a report of their research in the form of a thesis.

Postgraduate diploma

If students enrolled in a postgraduate diploma programme are required to carry out an individual research project, the expectations are similar to those of an honours research project and thesis. On the other hand, postgraduate diploma students are sometimes encouraged or required to become involved in a group research project that has been devised by a member (or perhaps two or three members) of the academic staff of the department. Usually, such group projects are designed in very general terms only. Apart from designing the project at a general level, the expectations of the students in the group are similar to those applicable to an individual research project. In particular, students are required to write individual theses.

Masters and professional doctorates

At masters and professional doctorate levels, the requirements of the research component of the programme are similar to those at honours level. However, because students at this level will previously have carried out a research project and written a thesis at honours or postgraduate diploma level, a higher standard of work and more originality will be expected.

▶ The research

In any programme of study, the effort that can be devoted to the research component is limited by the time available and the need to work concurrently on coursework – and research is time-consuming. Therefore, the research carried out by students must be limited in scope. On the other hand, this does not mean that the research should be overly limited or simple. As a guide, at honours and post-graduate diploma levels the research involved will usually be similar in scope to that reported in a journal article that involves a single and relatively small experiment or study. By comparison, at masters and professional doctorate levels the research should be similar to that reported in a major journal article – possibly involving multiple experiments or studies.

Individual research projects

Students who are working on an individual research project are typically required to identify the research problem[6] and define a specific research question to investigate. In addition, they are required to design and carry out the necessary research. They are, therefore, expected to collect their own data. However, if the research involves the collection of a very large volume of data, it might be permissible for a student to be given help. For instance, it might be acceptable for teachers to assist with the collection of data from children, but the student would be required personally to collect at least a substantial proportion.

Although they may be given advice on data analysis, students must choose appropriate techniques and analyse the data collected. Where appropriate, this includes the testing of hypotheses.

Group research projects

When students are involved in a group research project, it is most likely that they will be presented with a research problem, and they might be given a specific research question to investigate. The form of research might be given in general terms, or effectively be determined by the nature of the research problem. On the other hand, it is most likely that students will have to design the research in detail.

It is typically a requirement that individual students' research must differ in some way. Usually, this means that individual students will investigate some particular aspect of the research problem, perhaps in addition to some common aspect. Therefore, when designing the research, it might be necessary to include additional variables to cater for individual students' needs. For example, the inclusion of such a variable might be needed to allow a student to test some hypothesis.

The students must collect the necessary data. Of course, no one student will collect all of the data: this task will be shared equally among the group.

Members of the group will enter the data that they collect into a common data file. When this is completed, individual students must analyse the group data. It is not acceptable for one student to carry out the data analysis for the group. In any event, because it is likely that there will be some differences between students' research projects, it can be expected that there will be a need for individual data analyses.

When some common data analysis is required (e.g., when testing a group hypothesis), although they may be given advice, the selection of appropriate techniques is a group responsibility. Similarly, the selection of suitable techniques needed for individual analyses (e.g., testing of individual hypotheses) is the responsibility of the student involved.

▶ Documenting the research

Put simply, a thesis presents an account of a piece of original research that has been carried out by a student. It must demonstrate that there is a valid research problem that is of some importance, describe how it was investigated, and present the results of that investigation. In particular, it must present an interpretation of the outcome of the research and its implications, and offer a solution or partial solution to the research problem addressed.

Group research projects

Individual theses are also required in the case of a group research project. Although there will be similarities between the theses of group members, there will also be differences. Obviously, there will be variation in areas such as the organization of material and manner of expression, use of sources, and ideas presented. In addition, differences are likely to result from the requirement to investigate an individual aspect of the research problem and, where applicable, the need to test individual hypotheses.

Length of the thesis

Departments set length limits for theses, and these vary with the programme of study. At honours level, the length of a thesis is typically in the order of about 10,000–15,000 words, while at postgraduate diploma level the length might be somewhat shorter. By comparison, at masters or professional doctorate levels the allowed length is likely to be longer – perhaps in the order of 20,000–25,000 words.

On the other hand, in some programmes students are not required to submit a conventional thesis. Rather, they are required to submit what is essentially a substantial journal article, and so the allowed length will be considerably shorter than those suggested above. When this is so, some departments require the separate submission of a substantial literature review that is likely to be in the order of about 6000 words.

▶ Two-part research components

In some programmes, the research component is divided into two parts that are variously referred to as courses, subjects, modules, or units. When this is so, students are required in the first part to write a formal research proposal,[7] and in the second they carry out the research and write their theses. However, it is important to understand that the research component remains as an entity. It is only nominally divided into two parts to help students to manage their work and to ensure that they have devised suitable research projects before they embark upon them.

Usually, in this situation the research proposal is expected to include a comprehensive literature review, and so it will be quite lengthy – perhaps in the order of about 7000–8000 words. If a conventional thesis is required, this literature review is essentially duplicated in its introduction – although no doubt in a somewhat revised form. On the other hand, if the thesis is required to be in the form of a journal article, its introduction will comprise only an abbreviated version of the literature review included in the research proposal.

► Motivation

Some students do not fully appreciate the benefits that accrue to them as a result of devising and carrying out a research project and writing a thesis. As a result, they approach the research component of their study as simply a "hurdle to be jumped". This is unfortunate because, apart from the personal benefits that are derived from it, research can be an exciting and rewarding activity. Most people enjoy an intellectual challenge. For example, some like solving crossword puzzles and some, playing a game of chess; others like reading a mystery novel and trying to identify the culprit.

Research is problem solving. For instance, carrying out research is rather like trying to solve a murder mystery. The problem is identified (who committed the murder), an investigation is carried out, clues gathered, and logical reasoning (based on the evidence collected) is used to produce an answer.

If you approach the research component of your study with a positive attitude, appreciate the benefits that will accrue to you, and view your research as an intellectual challenge, then you will most likely find that you enjoy the exercise and that you will achieve a sense of satisfaction from it. You might even find, as have many students, that you enjoy research so much that you will subsequently become an active researcher.

2 Time

Time is perhaps the most important consideration when enrolling in a programme of study that includes a research component. Devising and carrying out a piece of research requires considerable time, and so does writing a thesis. Therefore, before you enrol in a programme, you must be sure that you understand what is involved and that you can devote the necessary time to the required work.

The time that you will need to devote to devising and carrying out your research, and to writing your thesis will vary with a number of factors. These include the contribution of the research component to the programme, the expected comprehensiveness of the literature review, and the complexity of the research involved. As an example, however, in a one-year honours programme that follows from a three-year undergraduate degree, or in the final year of a three- or four-year honours programme, the research component usually contributes 50%. In such a programme – which is actually of about 9–10 months duration – you can expect that the research component will involve about 4–5 months of work. This equates to about 20 hours of work per week, but the time required in a given week will vary with stages of the research and of thesis writing.

In the case of postgraduate diploma, masters, or professional doctorate programmes, the time that needs to be devoted to the research component will vary with its contribution to the programme, and a calculation similar to that used above for an honours programme is appropriate. However, if the research component is divided over 2 years (as it is sometimes in masters and professional doctorate programmes) the time involved will be spread over both.

Apart from that needed for the research component of the programme in which you enrol, you will also have to devote time to the coursework component. In addition, it is likely that you will be in paid employment of some form, and you will have personal commitments such as family activities, hobbies, sport, and perhaps other obligations.

Whatever your situation, before you enrol in a programme of study you must think about the time that you have to devote to it. This means that you will have to consider the time that you devote to other commitments. In some cases, you might have to defer some activities or perhaps withdraw temporarily from some. You will also have to take into account the time involved before committing yourself to any new activity or taking a vacation during the period of your study.

It is critical that you fully appreciate the time commitment involved in the research component of a programme of study before you enrol in it. There is no point in later complaining that you did not appreciate the time required, or that some other commitment (including any associated with paid employment) interfered with your work on your research and thesis.

▶ Time frame

Regardless of whether or not it is divided into two parts, in an honours or postgraduate diploma programme the research component must be completed within 1 year. At the beginning of the year, it can be expected that about 1 month will be involved in deciding on an area of research and arranging supervision. It can then be expected that about 3–4 months will be involved in preliminary work, about 2–3 months in collecting data, and about 2–3 months in analysing and interpreting the outcome and finalizing the thesis. These estimates will, of course, vary with the nature of the research and thesis.

If the research component of a masters or professional doctorate programme must be completed within 1 year, the time frame involved will be similar to that for an honours or postgraduate diploma programme. On the other hand, sometimes the research component is divided into two parts (variously described as courses, subjects, modules, or units) and spread over 2 years. In the first part, students devise and design their research and submit a formal research proposal. In the second, they carry out the research and write their theses. For such a programme, it can be expected that, as for an honours or postgraduate diploma programme, about 3–4 months will be involved in preliminary work. After this is completed, writing the research proposal and gaining ethics approval will probably involve at least 2-month's work. Then, in the second year, about 2–3 months will be involved in collecting data, and about 2–3 months in analysing and interpreting the outcome, and finalizing the thesis.

▶ Deadlines

A due date for submission of a thesis will always be set. In addition, if a formal research proposal is required, a due date for submission of this will be set; and, if you are required to present your research proposal at a seminar, you will be given a date on which you are required to do so.

Apart from such deadlines, your supervisor might suggest the time by which other tasks should be completed. For example, it is likely that he or she will suggest a date by which data collection should be completed, and dates by which you should submit drafts of parts of your thesis.

▶ Time management

Because you will be working concurrently on your research, thesis, and coursework, and you will have other commitments in your life, you will have to manage your time carefully. The first step in doing this is to consider your own strengths and weaknesses in this regard. People often procrastinate, especially when the task involved is difficult. Some do this more than others do. If you are in this category, you will have to do something to overcome your tendency to procrastinate. For example, you might arrange regular meetings with your supervisor to force yourself to maintain steady progress.

▶ Planning time

You will have to plan your time so that you can comply with any deadlines given to you. Apart from this, you will need to plan time for your research so that you can ensure that any necessary resources are available when you need them. For example, you might need to arrange for the availability of some apparatus and for laboratory space or a room in which to test participants. In addition, you will usually need to arrange for participants, respondents, or subjects to be available when you need them.

The following advice is based on a research component in the form of a single item to be completed in 1 year, but it is equally applicable (with minor modification) to one that is divided into two parts, and possibly spread over 2 years.

Initially, you will only be able to plan your time in outline, but it is nonetheless necessary to do so. You will know the due date for submission of your thesis and any other deadlines that have been set. In addition, you should know at an early stage the due date for submission of any coursework assignments in the first semester and, at least approximately, the dates of any examinations involved. You will also know the dates of any employment or personal commitments. Therefore, you should be able to plan your time in the form of a schedule of events including, at this initial stage, the tentative dates for completion of major stages of your research.

As you advance with planning your research and set target dates for completion of each task involved, you can add this detail to your schedule of events. Similarly, you can add target dates for completion of the writing of the parts of your thesis.

You can plan your time using one of the commonly available time planners or, more preferably, by preparing a spreadsheet. In the latter case, you can have columns (or rows, if you prefer to work horizontally) for deadlines for completing stages of your research, writing parts of your thesis, due dates for coursework assignments and dates of examinations, employment commitments, and personal commitments. Planning your time in this way provides you with a visual representation of the ongoing and concurrent tasks and commitments that will be involved in the period during which you are working on your research and thesis. Moreover, it allows you to detect readily any clashes that might be involved. If any such clashes become evident, you will need to modify your plan to cater for them.

An example of part of a time plan, which illustrates a possible format, is shown in Box 1. The months, week numbers, and content of this example are intended for illustrative purposes only. Dates in the form of week ending or week beginning could be used in lieu of, or in addition to, week numbers. Notice how this example time plan shows a possible clash in week 18.

Box 1 Example format of a time plan

Month	Week	Research Thesis	Coursework	Personal	Employment
May	17		Essay due for PSY404		
	18	Finalize research design			Working on weekend
	19	Submit research proposal		Dad's birthday party	
	20	Complete first draft of introduction			
	21				Working on weekend
June	22	Complete pilot study			
	23		Exam week		
	24		Exam week		
	25	Complete second draft of introduction			

▶ **Target dates**

Planning time requires that you set target dates for completion of the various stages of your work. To do this, you will have to work backwards from any deadlines given to you – allowing time for completion of each stage of your work – and set target dates that will allow you to complete all of the necessary work within the time available.

Target dates must be realistic: There is no point in setting one that is so early that it is unachievable. On the other hand, target dates must not be set too late. You must allow time for the next stage of your work so that it can be completed before the target date set for that stage.

Commonly, completion of any task takes much longer than anticipated. In addition, unexpected events do occur. For example, a delay might be involved in gaining ethics approval for the research, a problem might arise in relation to arranging for participants to be available at a convenient time, or you might discover a problem with apparatus.

As an example, one student was carrying out research that involved measuring reaction and movement time. When he began to test children in a school, he found that the timers used in the apparatus were in error. He then ceased data collection, took the apparatus back to the university, and asked a technician to test it. This was done but no fault could be found. The student then returned to the school with the apparatus and began to collect data once more. Again, however, the previously observed errors became evident. Once more, the student returned the apparatus to the university for testing, but still no fault could be found. By this time, both the student and the technician were becoming somewhat frustrated. Fortunately, someone pointed out that, because no problem had been found with the apparatus during a pilot study at the university and no fault could be found when it was tested at the university, the problem must be associated with the school. Subsequent testing showed that the mains voltage at the power point in the school was less than the standard 240 volts, and further testing of the apparatus revealed that reducing the voltage below 240 resulted in errors in the timers being used. Steps were then taken to solve this problem.

The point of this anecdote is that the unexpected problem encountered with the apparatus resulted in the student involved losing over a week of his allocated data collection time. Moreover, he had to find replacements for the participants whom he had tested. While being realistic, therefore, when setting target dates you should allow a "fudge factor". For example, if you think that you can complete a task by a given date, set the target date some time earlier. This allows for the task involved taking longer to complete than anticipated, and for unexpected contingencies. If you complete a task early there is no problem, but if you complete it late there is.

Two series of target dates are required, one for the research and one for writing. There will be some overlap between these.

The research

If your research involves only a single experiment or study, the target dates that you will need to set are those for completion of

- the literature search,
- designing the research,

- pilot research,
- data collection, and
- data analysis.

Notes:

1. In the case of a piece of research that involves a pilot or validation experiment or study, you will need to set target dates for completion of data collection and analysis for this research, and for the research proper.
2. If the research involves multiple experiments or studies, you will need to set target dates for completion of the relevant steps for each.

Writing

A thesis can be divided into three parts: the introduction, the report of the research, and the discussion. The target dates that you will need to set for the writing part of your work, therefore, are those for completion of the

- introduction,
- report of the research,
- discussion, and
- finalization of the thesis.

Notes:

1. The introduction should preferably be written in close to its final form before beginning data collection.
2. If the piece of research involves pilot research that is to be reported separately, validation research, or multiple experiments or studies, target dates for completion of writing these parts of the thesis should be set.

▶ Estimating time

To allow you to set target dates for the completion of the stages of your research and the writing of your thesis, you will have to estimate the time needed for the various tasks involved. There is an old rule for planning the time required for a task: Estimate the time needed, double it, and add 50% to allow for contingencies. Tasks always take longer than expected, and you need to remember Murphy's Law: If something can go wrong, it will.

The literature search

It will always be impossible to read all of the literature that is potentially relevant to a given research problem. Therefore, you will have to allot time to this task.

A point that you should appreciate is that inevitably some sources that you want to consult will not be available in your library and so will have to be found elsewhere. This takes time. You should, therefore, begin searching the literature as soon as possible.

The research

Estimating the time needed to carry out research is difficult, and invariably some unforeseen problem arises. Nonetheless you must make some estimate of the time needed.

The first consideration is the time needed to gain ethics approval. You are not permitted to begin to collect data until this has been granted. Therefore, you must submit your application for ethics approval early enough to allow you to begin collecting data when you have planned to do so. When planning time for ethics approval, you need to consider the dates on which the ethics committee meets. You also need to allow time for the eventuality that provision of some additional information or changes to your research design might be required. This can sometimes result in a delay until the committee's next meeting.

In the case of experimental research, you can calculate the time needed for data collection. However, in other forms of research you will only be able to allot time to a task. For instance, in survey or qualitative research you might simply have to set a deadline by which data collection must be completed.

A point that is easy to overlook is that you need to prepare information letters to give to participants or respondents, and consent forms for participants to sign. Preparing and printing these takes time. You will need to plan for this so that the necessary information letters and consent forms are available when needed.

In survey research, you will typically need to prepare and print a questionnaire. Again, you will have to plan the necessary time so that the required number of questionnaires is available when needed. In addition, you will have to consider the time needed for questionnaires to be distributed to respondents, and for them to complete and return them. You will have to set target dates for distribution of questionnaires and for completion of data collection. The latter is especially important. You cannot keep waiting and hoping for more questionnaires to be returned.

A particular consideration when planning time is that needed for analysis and interpretation of the data collected. It is very easy to underestimate the time needed for this. Data analysis often proves not to be as straightforward as was anticipated. In addition, interpretation of the outcome of research often presents unforeseen difficulties.

Writing

Writing a thesis always requires much more time than is initially anticipated. You will encounter periods of "writer's block" when you find that you can write little of anything. In addition, you will have coursework to complete, and no doubt employment and personal commitments. You will not, therefore, be able to set aside a block of time that is long enough to write your thesis in its entirety in "one sitting". Even if you could, you might well find that some unexpected contingency precludes you from writing during the time that you set aside. Consequently, you will find that you have to write your thesis in parts over a considerable period.

When planning time for writing, always allow time for writing and editing a number of drafts. In addition, allow time for your supervisor to read drafts: he or she cannot simply "drop everything" to read them. Moreover, you should work on the assumption that your supervisor will make suggestions for changes. You must, therefore, allow time for revision of drafts.

Figures, tables, and appendices

If you are wise, you would have prepared any necessary figures, tables, and appendices as you wrote the individual parts of your thesis. However, when you have completed the writing and printing of the parts, you will have to insert figures and tables at appropriate points, and add the appendices. You need to allow time for doing this.

The preliminary pages

After you have completed all else, you will have to prepare the necessary preliminary pages (i.e., the title page, table of contents, and so on) Again, this takes time and you need to allow for this.

Final proofreading

When you have completed your thesis and printed the final version, you have to proofread it in its entirety. By the time that you have reached this point, you will no doubt be experiencing some stress, and you will probably want to "get it all over with". It is, therefore, easy to overlook something, and so you need to take the time to make a final check of your thesis, and to rectify any flaws that you detect – such as having inserted a figure in the wrong place. You must allow time for this.

Binding

Finally, when you have completed all else, you will have to make the required number of copies of your thesis and to have these bound. This takes time, particularly if you are required to have your thesis professionally bound. In addition, other students will be having their theses bound at about the same time, which can result in a delay. Again, you must allow for this.

▶ Thinking

Always allow time for thinking. Too often, this is overlooked. Much academic work involves "sitting and thinking". For instance, you have to think analytically and critically about material that you read. You also have to think about, for example, how you can manipulate some independent variable or measure the dependent variable, or how to organize material in some part of your thesis. If you do not allow time for thinking, you can encounter problems. A typical example is that students tend to plan time for data analyses on the basis of how long it will take to calculate some statistic, but they fail to allow time for thinking about and interpreting the outcome.

▶ Monitoring your work

There is no point in planning your work if you do not follow that plan as closely as possible. It is critical that you monitor your progress to ensure that you do not fall behind. On the other hand, you can only plan on the basis of the information available to you. For example, when you plan your time early in the year you will not know the due dates for submission of coursework assignments later in the year, and unexpected events do arise. In addition, estimates of the time needed to complete tasks often prove not to be correct. You will, therefore, find it necessary to change your time plan as the year progresses.

Changing your time plan does not mean simply changing target dates. Presuming that you originally planned your time carefully, there will not be a great deal of flexibility in the target dates that you have set. If you made a reasonably accurate estimate of the time required for a given task, you cannot simply reduce the time allowed for it. Rather, you will have to consider carefully all of your commitments and the time allotted to each. Then you will have to make appropriate adjustments. In any event, you must always work back from the due date for submission of your thesis, and ensure that you can complete the necessary work by that time.

▶ Some advice

If you appreciate that devising and carrying out a piece of research, and writing a thesis involves a considerable commitment, plan your time carefully, and monitor your progress, you should be able to complete the required work comfortably within the time available. Sometimes, unexpected events occur that result in delays, but if you have taken this possibility into consideration when planning your time you should be able to "catch up". On the other hand, sometimes an unexpected event, such as serious illness, can detract very markedly from the time available to a student.

If you fall behind schedule at any time during your work on your research and thesis, you should discuss the problem with your supervisor as soon as possible. Do not hesitate to ask for help. Often, your supervisor will be able to offer some advice to help you to overcome the problem. In any event, do not simply wait and hope that the problem will disappear. If you delay asking for advice, you might find that it is "too late".

3 Considerations

Before beginning to work on a research project and thesis, you need to understand what is involved. There are differences between programmes of study, and in requirements and policies between departments. You must familiarize yourself with the requirements of the programme of study in which you are enrolled, and with the policies of the department and university in which you are studying. Typically, you will be given a handbook in which these are detailed.

Of necessity, such handbooks include a lot of information of an administrative nature, and details such as the requirements for presentation and binding of the thesis. At this early stage, much of such content will be of little interest to you, and far from exciting. On the other hand, you will find that the handbook typically also includes useful advice and some pearls of wisdom. You will, therefore, have to read it carefully, taking note of that which is of immediate importance, and ensuring that you are aware of other content for future reference. Then you should discuss any questions that arise with the staff member who is the programme co-ordinator.

A limitation of the handbooks given to students is that, because of the wide variety of possible research projects and theses, it is impossible to include all of the advice that an individual student might need: only a student's supervisor can offer specific advice. The problem is that students need some advice that typically is not included in handbooks before they enter into a supervisory arrangement. This chapter, therefore, provides some background information and offers some generic advice to help you at this initial stage.

▶ Some general advice

If you are enrolled in an honours or postgraduate diploma programme of study, it is most likely you will not previously have carried out a research project and written a thesis. Consequently, having familiarized yourself with what is involved, you are likely to face the task ahead with some trepidation and some doubt about how to approach it. Some advice, therefore, may be of help.

Volume of work

Students who have not previously devised and carried out a research project and written a thesis are commonly daunted by the volume of work involved, and it is likely that you will be no exception. However, if you think of what you need to do as a series of tasks that you need to accomplish, you will see the prospect as being much more feasible. It is rather like looking up at a steep hill that you have to climb and thinking that you can never reach the top. If, instead of concentrating on the top of the hill, you think of reaching first that tree, and then that large rock, and so on, you will find that the task becomes perceptually manageable, and you will get to the top with what seems to have been not a great deal of effort. The same applies to thinking about what is involved in a research project and thesis.

Skills and abilities

Another problem that sometimes arises is that, having familiarized themselves with what they must achieve, honours and postgraduate diploma students lack confidence in their ability to do so. However, there should be no need for worry.

Before you enrol in a programme of study that includes a research component, you will have studied a range of areas in psychology, and so you will be familiar with the discipline. More specifically, you will have written papers such as essays and research reports. Therefore, you will be familiar with what is involved in seeking out relevant literature and evaluating it, and you should be able to synthesize material, and to think analytically and critically. In addition, you will have studied research methods and data analysis, and you will have had some exposure to both. You will, then, have the knowledge, abilities, and skills needed to identify a research problem, design and carry out a piece of research to investigate it, analyse the data collected, interpret the outcome, and write a thesis.

You should understand that the reason for inclusion of a research component in a programme of study is to allow you to further develop your existing skills and abilities and, in particular, your knowledge of research in general. Therefore, you are not expected to be able to devise and carry out a completely independent research project. Rather, you will do so under supervision.

Given your pre-existing skills and abilities, and the guidance of your supervisor, you should find that the research component of your programme of study will not be unduly difficult. It will, of course, require considerable time and work. However, you will derive a sense of achievement and more than a little satisfaction from your efforts.

Group research projects

If you become involved in a group research project, you are committing yourself to the group and to the associated responsibilities. In particular, you must be willing to maintain frequent contact with other group members and, put colloquially, "pull your weight". You must also be willing to comply with any target dates set by the group for completion of tasks. If you fail in your obligations, other members of the group will be penalized. Therefore, if you are not prepared to commit yourself to the group and its goals, you should not become involved in a group research project.

▶ Individual vs group research projects

In most programmes of study, students are required to carry out an individual research project; but, in some, they are encouraged or required to carry out a group research project. Before offering any further advice, therefore, what is involved in individual and group research projects needs to be outlined.

Individual research projects

Most commonly, students who are involved in an individual research project arrange supervision with a particular academic, and in some departments it is a prerequisite for students to do so before they are allowed to enrol. Such arrangements are made on the basis of the student's interests and the area of expertise of the academic involved.

Sometimes, students are allocated to a supervisor – usually because they have not arranged supervision and other academics are not available. When this happens, students are likely to find that their choice of an area in which to work is limited by that in which their supervisors have expertise. In this case, it might be that the academic involved has already devised a research project on which he or she would like a student to work. The problem with this is that the student can sometimes become virtually an unpaid research assistant. Consequently, while gaining experience in research, the opportunity for the student to demonstrate his or her own creativity and originality is limited.

More typically, when assigned to a supervisor, students are expected to identify the research problem that they will investigate within the area in which their supervisors have expertise. If you find yourself in this situation, the major problem that you will encounter is that you will be lacking in background knowledge, and possibly interest. On the other hand, you will have the advantage that your supervisor will have expertise in the area. Moreover, you are likely to find that, as you read in the area and develop a familiarity with it, you will develop an interest in it.

Expertise

Although he or she does not have expertise in the area, an academic might be prepared to supervise a research project in one of the student's choice. In this case, the academic can offer helpful advice and guidance of a generic nature in areas such as research design and the writing of the thesis. However, he or she might not be familiar with some research techniques that are commonly used in the area. For example, not all academics are intimately familiar with qualitative research techniques. Moreover, it is likely that the academic involved will not be familiar with the literature in the area and so his or her ability to offer advice in the matter of the literature search will be limited.

In some instances, a student enrols in a programme of study with a particular research project in mind, but then finds that no academic in the department has expertise in the area. When this happens, the student might well find that no academic in the department is willing to supervise him or her. If the student still insists on working on that project, and can find a willing supervisor, he or she will have to accept the limitations to supervision that are involved.

If you want to work on a specific research project, you should consider the areas of expertise of the staff of the department of the university in which you intend to enrol. You may already be familiar with the staff in the department; but, if you are not, you can usually find a list of the areas of interest of staff members in a handbook given to prospective students or on the university's Website. Presuming that you know of, or find, a staff member who has expertise in the area in which you want to work, you should discuss the possibility of supervision with that person. If there is no prospective supervisor who has expertise in the area, you might be well advised to consider enrolling in a university in which a staff member does have the necessary expertise.

Group research projects

Sometimes, students are encouraged or required to carry out a group research project that has been devised by an academic, or perhaps two or more, in the department. It may be that more than one such project is offered. In this case, students may be allocated to a group and so to a research project, or they may be given the option of choosing from those that are offered.

When group research projects are offered, it can be expected that the research problem and usually the research question to be investigated will be at least largely predetermined. In addition, the research design may be given (in general terms), or essentially determined by the nature of the research problem and question. It remains, however, that the research problem and question must be defined, and the research must be designed in detail by the students in the group in consultation with the academic(s) supervising the project.

If students' research projects must differ, as is typically the case, individual students are likely to be required to investigate an individual research question, perhaps in addition to a common research question. In the case of experimental research, this is likely to involve the testing of individual hypotheses, perhaps in addition to some common hypothesis or hypotheses. When this is so, students develop their individual variation on the common research design in consultation with the academic(s) involved.

▶ Originality

The research problem investigated need not be particularly novel. On the other hand, its investigation must be novel in some way, and involve some originality. It is not acceptable, merely, to replicate a published experiment or study. Similarly, it would not be acceptable to make only a minor modification to research that has been reported in the literature. As an example, if a published journal article reported the result of an experiment testing a response at 5 and 10 seconds, it would not be acceptable virtually to replicate this experiment by testing the same response at say 5, 10, and 15 seconds. Simply extending research in this way does not constitute originality. By comparison, it might be acceptable to modify a previously reported experiment or study by introducing a new variable, or by manipulating or measuring a variable in a different way.

One student's method of presenting stimuli in an experiment provides an example of an acceptable modification of previous research. He found that a previous investigator had tested the accuracy of judgment of line lengths by presenting four stimulus lines (drawn on alternate sides of an octagonal piece of wood) shown in an aperture. The student presented stimulus lines on a video monitor, under computer control. This allowed for the use of more stimulus line lengths. More importantly, it allowed for the random variation of the start point (and so the end point) of the lines, which was not possible in the research carried out by the previous investigator.

The research reported in a masters or professional doctorate thesis should show more originality than that in an honours or post-graduate diploma thesis. Research at this level would be expected to show originality in regard to the research problem or question, and/or adopt a new approach to its investigation.

▶ Quantitative vs qualitative research

Most commonly, students carry out research of a quantitative nature, and collecting data in research of this type (whether experimental or non-experimental) is usually straightforward, as is analysis of the data. On the other hand, there can sometimes be problems. Often, these can be detected and rectified as the result of pilot research. It is, however, always advisable to carry out a research project that is unlikely to present any unexpected problems. In particular, it is wise to carry out a project that involves data collection and analysis techniques with which you are familiar.

Some students embark on a research project of a qualitative nature because this form of research appeals to them, and some because investigation of the research problem in which they are interested requires this form of research. On the other hand, some students choose qualitative research because they lack confidence in their knowledge of statistics. Therefore, they tend to think that, because it usually does not employ statistical analysis, qualitative research will be easier than quantitative research.

Designing qualitative research and collecting the necessary data can present difficulties, and unexpected problems often arise. In addition, typically a very large volume of data is collected and the necessary analysis can be complex and time-consuming. Put simply, qualitative research can prove to be much more difficult than quantitative research.

▶ Theoretical basis

Most commonly, research is designed to test a hypothesis that has been derived from some theory. In any event, research is typically guided by some theory that provides a perspective from which to view the research problem, or a framework within which to investigate it. For instance, theory can suggest what variables are relevant, what relationships might be involved, and how the data collected might be interpreted.

Often, theory can be useful when investigating an applied problem. As an example, one honours student had noticed that when assembling an item, her father seemed to be able to do so more easily when following pictorial as contrasted with written instructions. She was able to investigate this problem by relating it to information processing theory. On the other hand, theory is often less central in applied research, and particularly in qualitative research. This is not, however, to be taken to suggest that such research should be atheoretical: rather, it should be based upon theory, or carried out to add to some existing theory or to develop a new theory. Research that is not based upon or does not contribute to the development of a theory is of little value.

▶ Goals of scientific research

It is important to understand that the scientific approach involves more than simply gathering information. Science is goal-directed. In particular, it is directed to produce the solution to the research problem being investigated. You need, then, to understand that the

goals of scientific investigation are to describe and explain, preferably predict, and – if possible – to offer the prospect of control. It
follows that a thesis that is merely descriptive in nature is of little
value.

▶ Outcome

In the case of experimental research, it is not critical that the hypotheses developed are supported by the results. However, students
must demonstrate the ability to devise suitable hypotheses, design
and carry out research to test these, select and use appropriate statistical techniques to analyse the data collected and test the hypotheses involved, and interpret correctly the outcome.

Qualitative research may not involve the testing of explicit hypotheses. On the other hand, it must have some clear direction and
purpose. Commonly, therefore, although not in the form of a conventional hypothesis, there will be some expectations with regard to
the outcome. In any event, students must demonstrate the ability to
analyse appropriately the data collected, and to offer a valid interpretation of the outcome.

Regardless of the form of research involved, it must be designed
to provide an answer to the specific research question being investigated and, by doing so, provide a solution or partial solution to the
research problem being addressed. In addition, it should be designed
to achieve the scientific goals of description and explanation, preferably prediction, and ideally control. The research must *not* result in
a thesis that is merely descriptive in nature.

▶ Documenting the research

Regardless of whether students are carrying out an individual or a
group research project, individual theses must be written. You will
be given details of the expectations and requirements for a thesis in
the programme of study in which you are enrolled. However, it is a
good idea to read two or three example theses written by previous
students. Copies of those that have been submitted in the past will
be held in the university library, and often in a department library.

Reading two or three example theses will give you a good idea of
the task that you face – in terms of both the research involved and the
thesis. However, you need to understand that there is a wide variety

of possible research projects, and theses differ widely in content and structure. No single thesis, therefore, will provide a model that you can follow.

► Supervision

It is important for you to understand what is involved in supervision so that you know what to expect and what is expected of you. While academics differ somewhat in their styles of supervision, the following outline is generally applicable.

Individual research projects

Departments vary in their policy with regard to supervision. Commonly, a single academic is responsible for supervising a student, but some departments have a policy of joint supervision. The latter is intended to ensure that supervision is available in the absence of a student's primary supervisor.

In some instances, external supervision might be advisable or necessary. When this is so, joint supervision may be arranged, and there will be both an external and an internal supervisor. Usually, the external supervisor is primarily responsible for advice and guidance on matters relating to the research project and writing of the thesis, while responsibility for advice on matters relating to the department and university requirements remains with the internal supervisor.

Regardless of the form of supervision involved, it is important to understand that a supervisor's role is to provide advice and guidance. It is *not* to ensure that a student completes a research project, writes a thesis, or achieves a particular grade. While supervisors will do their best to help students to overcome any problems that they encounter, all that they can do is to offer advice. It remains that the research project and the thesis are the *student's* responsibility.

It is also important to understand that you will need to maintain regular contact with your supervisor so that he or she can monitor your work and offer appropriate and timely advice and guidance. It is *your* responsibility to do this. Your supervisor is not responsible for maintaining contact with you.

To ensure that you progress satisfactorily and complete your thesis before the due date, your supervisor may set deadlines for completion of various parts of your research project and thesis. You should appreciate that any such deadlines will be set to help you. Again, it is *your* responsibility to comply with any deadlines that have been set. It is not your supervisor's responsibility to ensure that you do.

The assistance that your supervisor provides will be in the form of offering advice. You should not expect simply to be told "how to do it". Carrying out a research project and writing a thesis is a learning experience, but it is largely a "self-learning" one. Your aim should be to develop your existing skills and abilities – under the guidance of your supervisor – to the point that you can independently carry out a research project.

Group research projects

In principle, supervision of group research projects does not differ from supervision of individual research projects. There are, however, some practical differences.

Because it is a group research project, students must be supervised as a group. To achieve this, supervisors usually arrange group meetings at which those aspects of the research project that are common are discussed. In addition, there is typically a requirement for students' research projects to differ, and those aspects of the research that are specific to individuals will be discussed in individual meetings.

Maximizing the benefits

Whether you are working on an individual or a group research project, you should maximize the benefits available to you through the supervisory process. Make sure that you attend any meetings that have been arranged, and be on time. If there is some particular point that you want to discuss, or some problem with which you need help, give your supervisor advance notice so that he or she can give the issue some thought before the meeting. In any event, you should make notes of any issues that you wish to raise, so that you do not forget anything. Also, make sure that you make careful notes of the outcome of your discussions so that you can later refer to advice that has been offered.

Personality

A point that you should understand is that supervisors are actually human. Just like you, they will have personal opinions, attitudes, preferences, and so on. If you do not already know your supervisor, it is a good idea to "get to know" him or her, and to allow your supervisor to "get to know" you. Often, knowing one another can obviate a problem, such as a misunderstanding, that might otherwise occur. It is, therefore, a good idea to maintain regular contact with your supervisor, and to allow adequate time for meetings.

Typically, personality differences are not a problem in the supervisor–student relationship. On occasion, however, friction can arise. For instance, a student might come to believe that his or her supervisor is not offering adequate advice and guidance, or perhaps is being inconsistent. If you experience any such difficulty, your first step should be to discuss it openly and honestly with your supervisor. Often, difficulties of this nature are more in perception than reality, and so discussing the issue will usually lead to a solution.

If, after having discussed the problem with your supervisor, you cannot reach a suitable and amicable solution, you should discuss the issue with the co-ordinator of the programme of study. You should not, however, do this without giving your supervisor the courtesy of advising him or her of your intention.

▶ Problems and advice

The following advice is offered for an individual research project, but it is no less applicable to group research. The only difference is that the group has to function as an entity. On the other hand, where individual aspects of a group research project are involved, the advice offered here is applicable to individual students.

Solving problems

Inevitably, you will encounter problems as you progress through your work. When confronted with a problem, you should try to work out how you can solve it without assistance. For example, if you were trying to find a suitable method for the manipulation of some variable you should consider how previous researchers have done so. You can do this by reading previous research reports in the area. Similarly, if you were trying to select a suitable method for analysis of data, you can often find an appropriate one by reading previous research reports. On the other hand, you should not simply and slavishly follow what has been done before. Rather, you should think analytically and critically, and perhaps use some creativity. You might, for example, be able to devise a better method of manipulating some variable or see a better approach to data analysis.

Of course, it is not always possible to solve every problem that one encounters on one's own. It might be that all that one needs to do is to talk to someone about the problem. Perhaps surprisingly, sometimes in the process of explaining a problem to another, the solution suddenly becomes apparent. In other instances, the solution presents itself as a result of a question asked of one. For example, your supervisor might ask, "Have you considered ...?"

Attempting to overcome difficulties that you encounter will help you to become an independent problem solver. Moreover, if you solve some problems on your own, you are likely to find that your supervisor will inevitably be much more helpful with the fewer more difficult problems that you encounter. On the other hand, do not be too heroic. Seek help when you need it.

Taking advice

Solving a problem often involves taking advice, and your supervisor is your primary source. However, although he or she will try to help you to solve the problems that you will inevitably encounter, no one can solve your problems for you. All that can be done is to offer advice to help *you* to do so.

Sometimes, your supervisor will advise you to consult an article or a book, but you need to appreciate that such sources offer only ideas, not solutions. Moreover, you will often find differences between the ideas presented. When this is so, you must analytically and critically examine the ideas involved, and the evidence and reasoning upon which they have been developed. On this basis, you must decide which idea(s) to accept and which to reject.

Similarly, if your supervisor suggests that you consult someone who is an expert in an area, all that he or she can do is to offer advice. Moreover, if you consult more than one person you might well be given conflicting advice. This can arise because there are differences of opinion on some matters. For example, not everyone will agree on the interpretation of the outcome of some piece of research or the most appropriate techniques to use in a particular data analysis. The advice offered in this book is no exception: not everyone will agree with all of it. As for differences in ideas that you find in journal articles and books, when you are given conflicting advice you will have to weigh up that which has been given to you, and decide which to accept and which to reject.

You have to devise and carry out your research project, analyse the data, interpret the outcome, and write your thesis. All that anyone else can do is to offer you advice. The final decision is yours.

▶ The research

When considering possible research, there are some matters of a practical nature that you must consider.

Validation research

If your intended research involves the necessity to develop an instrument such as a scale for measuring some variable, this will obviously have to be validated before you can use it. The obvious problem is that this will take time. In addition, it might well be that you subsequently find that the instrument that you have devised is not valid. If this were to happen, you would have to redesign the instrument and carry out another validation study, which might also fail.

You would do well to consider carefully the advisability of carrying out any research that necessitates developing an instrument. Devising and validating an instrument typically constitutes a research project in its own right.

Difficult research

Some research is very difficult. This could, for example, result from the need for the development of some intricate apparatus, involved negotiation with an external organization, complicated data-collection procedures, or the need for complex data analyses.

It is not necessary for students' research projects to be unduly difficult, and it might well be that no credit is given for the difficulty involved when a thesis is ultimately examined. Put simply, you are well advised not to become involved in difficult research.

Dangerous research

In rare instances, research can be potentially dangerous. You are unlikely to consider research that involves any obvious danger. However, sometimes research can involve potential danger that might not be immediately obvious. For example, although perhaps small, there can be some risk involved in observing the behaviour of particular groups in some areas late at night, or in interviewing strangers in their homes. You must never consider becoming involved in any research that involves potential risk or danger. In any event, the university ethics committee would not approve of any potentially dangerous research.

Feasibility

Often, the research that students would like to carry out is simply not feasible within the time available. For instance, it might involve a long period of participant involvement, or preliminary testing followed after a lengthy interval by a post-test. As another example, it might be that individual testing would not require a great deal of time; but, because the research necessitates the participation of a very large number of people, collecting the data would require a lengthy study.

Sometimes, a supervisor might recommend that a research project should not be undertaken because it is likely to prove not to be feasible. In other instances, a supervisor might suggest a truncated or modified research design. Students can refuse to accept such advice, but they do so at their peril.

The feasibility of research must always be carefully considered before it is seriously contemplated further. This requires estimating the time needed; ensuring that any necessary resources are available; ensuring that suitable participants, respondents, or subjects are available; and considering any potential problems that might arise. In effect, you have to design your research in outline to allow you to assess its feasibility.

Participants, respondents, or subjects

The availability of participants, respondents, or subjects is critical. Often, this is not a problem. On the other hand, if some particular characteristic is required, there can be difficulties. For example, if you need participants who have some particular form of brain damage, you might not be able to find an adequate number. It is often difficult to find participants, even though the characteristic required is apparently quite common. For example, one student encountered difficulty with finding an adequate number of participants who were left-hand dominant.

In some instances, you will have to carry out preliminary testing to identify suitable participants. When this is so, you will need to consider the prevalence of the characteristic that is required, and so the number of people that you will need to test to find an adequate number for your research. In addition, you will have to estimate the time that will be required to carry out the necessary testing in order to identify an adequate number of participants.

Even if you can locate suitable people, they might not all be willing to take part in your research. Therefore, having identified suitable prospective participants, you need to ensure that they are willing to participate in your research – including any necessary preliminary testing. In addition, you need to ensure that they will be available when you need them. For example, first-year students are usually available only during teaching periods. Similarly, other participants will be available only at times that are convenient to them.

Availability of respondents in survey research is often not a problem. However, it can be if some particular characteristic, such as membership of some specific group, is required. The more likely problem is the commonly experienced low response rate when questionnaires are distributed by mail. It is, therefore, typically necessary to distribute quite a large number of questionnaires in order to achieve an adequate sample size, and this is likely to involve not inconsiderable time, effort, and cost.

Finding suitable and willing participants can sometimes be a particular problem in qualitative research. Such research often requires the involvement of a specific group of people, such as members of a religious sect or perhaps the survivors of a natural disaster. Before deciding on a research project that has any such requirement, you need to be confident that those in the group involved will agree to take part in your research.

Another consideration that can arise is that travel may be involved. For instance, it might be necessary for parents to bring children to the university, and they might not be willing to do so. More commonly, travel is a potential problem in qualitative research. For example, it is possible that the intended research involves a group of people who live in a place that is some distance from your location, and so you will have to travel to that place and perhaps be accommodated there for some time. When travel is necessary, you will have to consider the time and costs involved. In some instances, such considerations might result in an intended research project being impossible.

When research involves animal subjects, there is often no difficulty with obtaining them. For instance, presuming that the university has an animal laboratory, it is usually not difficult to obtain a sample of laboratory rats. On the other hand, it can sometimes be difficult, if not impossible, to find suitable subjects. This can arise, for instance, when the research involves animals that are usually found only in zoos. In this case, it might be that an adequate number of subjects are not available, or that a zoo will not grant permission for them to be used in the proposed research. Of course, carrying out research with animals in the wild presents obvious potential problems. In any case, you must ensure the availability of subjects when planning your research.

External organizations
Students sometimes want to work on a research project that requires the co-operation of an organization that is external to the university in which they are enrolled. For example, this might be a school, a business organization, or a hospital. Masters and professional doctorate students, in particular, might be interested in a specific research problem as a result of their employment – for instance, in a hospital or a commercial organization.

If the research that you are intending to carry out necessitates the co-operation of an external organization, you will have to give this careful consideration. For example, if you need access to patients in a hospital, members of the armed forces, animals in a zoo, or records in a database, you must be sure that this will be granted. It is highly unlikely, for instance, that a prison will allow students access to incarcerated criminals, or that a government department will allow access to confidential material.

When considering a research project that would necessitate the co-operation of an external organization, you must be confident that this will be provided. Before doing so, the organization will require details of your intended research. The problem is that you need to design your research in sufficient detail for the organization involved to consider it. If approval is not granted, you will have wasted a great deal of time and effort.

As an example, one masters student, who had served in the military, believed that he would be given approval to carry out research with service personnel, because he had been assured by an ex-colleague (who was still in the military) that he would be granted approval. However, after he had designed his research project and completed the required application documents, approval was denied. As a result, he had to discard his research project and to devise a new one. He was not well pleased.

Ethics

You will also need to consider ethical requirements. Sometimes, intended research is of such a form that it would not be approved by the university ethics committee. For example, it might involve asking questions of participants or respondents on sensitive matters (e.g., sexual behaviour) or some particular treatment of laboratory animals, and the ethics committee might not approve of the proposed research.

If your intended research requires the co-operation of an external organization, this will often require approval from the ethics committee of that organization, in addition to approval from the university ethics committee. Before you consider such research, you must be confident that the necessary ethics approval will be granted. Again, this raises the potential problem referred to above.

Apparatus and materials

In the case of experimental research that involves the use of apparatus, the department may or may not have it. If it does not, two questions arise: are funds available to purchase it, and is the department willing to do so? On the other hand, in some instances the necessary apparatus might not exist. If it does not, the question is: can it be made? Some departments have considerable resources, such as a workshop and technical and programming assistance, while others do not. Even when such resources are available, you need to appreciate that designing, making, and testing apparatus takes time. Therefore, you need to consider whether the required apparatus can be made within the available time.

If the research project that you are considering requires the use of some particular test, such as a personality inventory or an intelligence test, obviously it must be available. Departments will have a test library. However, there are many tests and the number held by a department is limited. Consequently, it might be that a particular test is not available. In this case again, the two questions arising are: are funds available to purchase it, and is the department willing to do so?

Regardless of the nature of resources that you need for your research, you must arrange for them to be available when needed. This means that you will have to take into consideration any time involved, such as that needed to obtain, or design and develop, the required resources.

▶ Other considerations

Unfortunately, there are some pragmatic considerations involved in research, and you need to consider them when devising a research project. Sometimes, consideration of these factors will reveal that an intended research project is not possible.

Legislation

It is likely that there will be some form of legislation in regard to privacy, which includes provisions for the collection, storage of, and access to information about individuals. In particular, there is likely to be legislation that precludes organizations from releasing certain information to third parties. For instance, this is very likely to be found in relation to criminal records or family court matters. Another consideration is that there might be a provision that precludes the collection of information from minors.

There is also likely to be legislation in regard to child protection. Typically, this will include a provision that precludes working with children unless a police check of some form has been carried out. This is likely to be so regardless, or whether or not, a parent or guardian is present during data collection.

Legal advice should be sought if there is any possibility of potential problems with regard to legislation. Seeking verbal advice from a government department is not sufficient. For instance, a staff member of a government department might suggest that carrying out particular research does not constitute "working with children" and that there should, therefore, be no problem. If a problem did eventuate, however, the individual giving that opinion and assurance is most likely to deny any responsibility, and to argue that he or she did not give a legal opinion.

Funding

Research sometimes requires funding. For example, it might be necessary to purchase an item of equipment or some test, or it might be that travel is involved and this must be paid for. A small amount of funding is usually available to students to assist with their research. Before committing yourself to a research project, however, you must be sure that any necessary funding is available.

Insurance

A point that is often overlooked is the possibility of loss of or damage to apparatus, equipment, or material being used in research. Universities have insurance policies to cover such eventualities. However, it is not always the case that the insurance will cover events that occur away from the campus. Therefore, it might not be acceptable to take apparatus, equipment, or material off campus. Another aspect of insurance to be considered is the possibility of personal injury occurring to a student or to participants during data collection or while travelling. Although very unlikely, the possibility does exist and it must be considered.

Usually, insurance is not a problem. On the other hand, it is important to ensure that that there is appropriate cover for participants, and that you do not put yourself at risk of any personal loss or litigation. This simply means that you need to know that appropriate insurance exists.

▶ A closing note

Unfortunately, the practicalities involved in the research component of a programme of study and the realistic purpose for which the research is carried out often obscure the intellectual purpose involved, which is to help students to develop their existing research skills and their knowledge of research in general. Of itself, however, research is goal-directed: it is carried out in the pursuit of knowledge, which is one of the greatest human traits – to quote Star Trek (including the split infinitive and sometimes perceived sexism), "To boldly go where no man has gone before." While practical considerations are of necessity involved, try not to think of your research project as simply another "hurdle to jump". Rather, try to think of it as climbing that mountain – just because it is there.

4 Preparation

Having familiarized yourself with the appropriate requirements and considerations, you have to carry out the initial preparation for your research project. What is involved in this will vary somewhat depending on whether you are required independently (albeit with the advice and guidance of your supervisor) to develop your research project, or you are constrained in some way. In particular, you might be restricted by the necessity to work in an area in which your supervisor has expertise, or you may be allocated to a supervisor and perhaps given a research project. If you are to become involved in a group research project, then you might be able to choose between two or more, or you might be allocated to a group.

The advice offered to you here is based on the assumptions that you are independently devising a research project. If you are not, then some of the advice offered will be superfluous. For example, if you are assigned to a supervisor no arrangement is required, and you might not have any choice in the area of research. In the case of a group research project, it is most likely that you will be given the research problem that is to be investigated.

▶ Initial preparation

Initial preparation for a research project involves six tasks. Although these are listed below separately, they are interrelated and should be thought of as parts of a single task.

1. Choose an area of research
2. Arrange supervision
3. Review the literature
4. Identify a research problem
5. Define the research problem
6. Define the research question

Area of research

Your first step is to decide on an area in which you would like to work. As an example, you might be interested in and familiar with cognitive psychology. Within this broad area, you need to identify a sub-area that particularly interests you. For instance, within the broad area of cognitive psychology you might be particularly interested in the function of memory, and so you would like to investigate some aspects of this.

Deciding on an area of psychology in which to work can be difficult if you are interested in more than one. In this case, it is a good idea to visit the library and to look at the research recently reported in two or three relevant psychology journals. It can also be helpful to look at theses that have recently been submitted to your department. Copies will be held in the library and, possibly, a department library. Reading reports of recent research can provide a stimulus to developing ideas.

Another guide to choice of research areas is the work of academics in the department. A list of their recent publications will usually be included in a handbook given to you for the research component of the programme of study, and it is likely that further information can be found on a department Website. In addition, it is a good idea to talk to some of the academics in the department about their current research interests. You might well find that that doing this leads you to a research project.

Group research projects

If you are required (or choose) to be involved in a group research project, and you are free to choose between two or more, you should choose one in an area in which you are interested and with which you are familiar. You should consider those projects offered and, if you are interested in more than one, discuss your interests and the project with the relevant staff member (or one of them if more than one is involved). On this basis, you will have to make a decision. However, there is no guarantee that you will be accepted into a particular group. It is most likely that some quota will have been set, and other students might already have arranged to work on the project.

Arranging supervision

When you have decided on an area in which you would like to work, you need to discuss your interests and the possibility of supervision with an academic in the department who has expertise in that area. However, you need to understand that for some reason a given academic might not be able to supervise you, or perhaps might not be willing to do so. In this case, you will have to arrange supervision with another academic who is available and willing.

You will find that academics are happy to discuss the possibility of supervision. Typically, they are keen to supervise students. Even if a given academic cannot supervise you, it is most likely that he or she will still be happy to discuss your research ideas with you. In this case, you might find that he or she will suggest that some other particular academic in the department would be likely interested in supervising you.

If you cannot be supervised by the academic of your first choice and no other academic in the department has expertise in the area in which you would like to work, two possibilities arise. Either you can be supervised by an academic who does not have expertise in the area and so can give you only generic advice and guidance, or you will have to work in an area in which an available supervisor has expertise. You might or might not have choice in this matter.

Departments typically have policies on supervision, and these may be included in a handbook given to students for a programme of study. In any event, you should discuss the relationship involved with your supervisor. If joint supervision is involved, you will need to ensure that you understand the role to be played by each supervisor.

Although it is likely to be far removed from your mind at this point, you should discuss with your supervisor his or her views and any departmental policies on subsequent publication of your work. This can obviate any misunderstanding or problems that might otherwise arise later.

Reviewing the literature

Because you will previously have written papers such as essays and research reports, you will be familiar with what is involved in a review of the relevant literature. In particular, you will be familiar with the searching of databases, narrowing the search, the type of literature that can be of use, and the need to evaluate critically the material that you read.

Seeking out and reading sources in the area of your intended research is likely to continue well into your preliminary work on your research. At this stage, however, you need to ensure that you are familiar with relevant theory, and with important ideas and previous research findings. What is involved in this will depend on your existing knowledge of the area. If you are familiar with it, you will already have a base of knowledge upon which to build: if you are not, then you will have to begin by reading general texts and possibly review articles to develop a base of knowledge upon which to build.

Identifying a research problem

Having ensured that you are familiar with the important literature, you have to identify a research problem to investigate. Students sometimes misunderstand the meaning of a research problem, often they are unsure of how to identify one that is important, and commonly they have difficulty with finding one. The following notes, therefore, are provided to help you in these areas.

The research problem

Problems in psychology include, for example, that how the brain functions, the nature of intelligence, the contribution of genetics to psychological disorders, and the functioning of memory, are not fully understood. However, such problems are what might be described as *macro* problems. They are too large to be investigated in any single piece of research. Rather, only some particular aspect of the problem can be addressed. Macro problems, therefore, are investigated at what might be described as the *micro* level. For example, a piece of research might be designed to examine how people recall information of a particular type. The outcome of such research can potentially provide one piece that can be put in its place in the "jigsaw puzzle", that is, the macro problem of the functioning of memory.

Microproblems arise frequently. For instance, there might be an inconsistency in the reported outcome of two experiments, or a possible alternative explanation of some research finding. The problems investigated in any single piece of research are of this form.

Importance of the research problem

To be of any value, the contribution of the outcome of research to human knowledge must be of some importance. It follows that any research problem being investigated must similarly be so. When used in this context, "importance" is not intended to involve value judgements. Nonetheless, to some extent such judgements are of necessity involved. For example, a research problem may not be "trivial", which implies a value judgement. It is, therefore, difficult to define "importance". As a guide, a research problem is important if

- its solution will support or question some theoretical position,
- it involves some human or animal behaviour that needs to be explained, or
- it has some practical application.

In contrast, a research problem is not important if

- it has already been thoroughly investigated and the solution is known,
- it is of no theoretical interest,
- the effect involved is known to be so small as to be immaterial, or
- there is no logical reason to be believed that the variables involved are related.

Although the research problem that you intend to investigate must be of some importance, it need not be greatly so. Rather, it should be modest and of a limited nature. You are not attempting to solve the world's problems, or even one of them. It is better to choose a research problem that involves relatively straightforward research. If you want to solve the world's problems, you are best advised to leave this to some time in your future career.

Finding a research problem
Students sometimes have a particular research problem in mind before they enrol in a programme of study. This could arise, for instance, as a result of having observed some problem in everyday life. An example of this is the student, referred to earlier, who had noticed that when assembling an item, her father seemed to experience difficulty with following written instructions. Another possibility is that a student might have a research problem in mind as a result of his or her employment. For instance, a student who is returning to study after an absence, and is enrolling in a masters or professional doctorate programme, might have developed an interest in a particular psychological disorder as a result of having been employed as a clinician.

More commonly, students do not have a specific research problem in mind. If you are in this position, you have to find one that you would like to investigate. You will already have decided on an area of psychology and within this, a specific sub-area in which you would like to work. Your task now is to find a research problem within that sub-area.

It is likely that you will have chosen an area of psychology on the basis of your previous study in the discipline. You might have found, for instance, that industrial and organizational psychology was particularly interesting. Presuming that this is so, as a starting point, you might like to scan through a textbook that you used, your lecture notes, or perhaps assignments that you wrote. Then, you should read journal articles and books in the area. Such reading is likely to lead to some aspect of the area in which you are interested, attracting your attention. As an example, you might find that you become interested in group performance. Limiting this further, you might find that you are intrigued by the effect of leadership on group performance.

Commonly, you will find research problems in the literature. For example, an author of an academic text might comment on an inconsistency between two theories, or suggest a flaw in some theory. Usually, however, research problems are found in published research reports. Investigators often suggest future lines of research. In addition, they might point out a flaw or weakness in their own research, or in that of some other investigator. This can lead to research in which an attempt is made to advance knowledge in the area.

Not all research problems, however, are found simply as a result of them having been explicitly pointed out in the literature. Rather, identifying a research problem usually results from careful analytical and critical thinking. For example, while reading the literature you might notice some inconsistency in research findings, think of an alternative explanation of some outcome, detect a flaw in an author's research or reasoning, or think of a new approach to the investigation of some problem.

Defining the research problem

Before you can begin to investigate a research problem, you must know exactly what you are trying to achieve. It follows that you must define the research problem clearly and precisely. For example, the problem that interests you could be that the effect of leadership in group functioning is not entirely clear. However, you must know exactly what aspect of this problem you intend to investigate. This might be, for instance, that the effect on group functioning of the level of intelligence of the leader is not well understood.

Defining the research question

There are always a number of research questions that could be investigated in the search for the solution to any given research problem. Therefore, having identified the research problem, you must define in clear and precise terms the research question that you intend to investigate. This is perhaps the most important part of your preparation, because the research that you carry out must have at least the potential to provide an answer to this question.

A research question is derived from a research problem. For example, if the problem addressed were that how memory functions is not fully understood, the question is, "How does memory function?" However, just as this problem is at the macrolevel, so too is the question. No single piece of research can provide the answer to such a question. On the other hand, a microproblem leads to a micro question. It might be, for example, that previous research suggests that rehearsal sometimes improves subsequent accuracy of recall, but that sometimes it does not. This presents a microproblem, and the resulting micro question could be, for instance, "Does accuracy of recall vary with the time allowed for rehearsal?" Such a question can readily be investigated.

It is important to understand that what is being specifically investigated in any research is the research question. While it is true that the research problem is being addressed, it is only a specific aspect of the problem that is being investigated – and this is the research question. In the example given above, for instance, it is possible to pose other questions such as, "Does familiarity with material similar to that to be remembered affect accuracy of recall?", or "Does perceived importance of the material affect accuracy of recall?"

▶ Research outline

When you have defined the specific research question that you intend to investigate, you need to design in outline the necessary research. For instance, if your research question were, "Does accuracy of recall vary with the time allowed for rehearsal?", you would need to design an experiment to investigate this. In this example, you would need to test the accuracy of recall of material by at least two groups of participants with varying time allowed for rehearsal in each group, or perhaps test the same group in two rehearsal-time conditions. You will, of course, have maintained frequent and regular contact with your supervisor, and so he or she should be familiar with your ideas and the direction in which you are moving. However, your supervisor will be engaged in a range of other activities, no doubt including the supervision of one or more other students. It is, therefore, unlikely that your supervisor will immediately be able to call to mind the detail of all of the discussions that you have had with him or her. It follows that you will need to present your supervisor with an outline of your research design before you progress further with your work. You must be confident that you have defined an appropriate research question and designed a suitable and feasible piece of research with which it can be effectively investigated.

Having assured yourself that you have devised a suitable piece of research in outline, you will then have to plan it in detail. This is covered in the next chapter, and it would be advisable for you to read that chapter before you evaluate your outline research design. At this point, however, without going into detail, you will need to consider some factors that can affect the feasibility of your intended research. Those that you will need to consider will vary with the nature of the research. Most commonly, however, they will include

1. resources needed;
2. nature and availability of participants, respondents, or subjects;
3. the number of participants, respondents, or subjects needed;
4. external organization involvement (if applicable);
5. ethics; and
6. the time needed to carry out the research.

Clearly, if your intended research involves, for example, the use of some apparatus or test that is not available, participants who are not available or not so in adequate numbers, or requires the co-operation of an external organization and this cannot be gained, it is not feasible. In such instances, you would have to abandon your intended research project and to find another.

Usually, ethical considerations do not present a problem in the research carried out by students, but sometimes it might be that they can result in a piece of research not being possible. You must, therefore, give some thought to ethical considerations at this point. It would be advisable for you to read Chapter 6, which covers this topic.

If you cannot complete your research within the time available, then it is not feasible. Sometimes, students are overly ambitious and they design a piece of research that simply cannot be completed in the time available. You must, therefore, make a reasonably accurate estimate of the time that will be involved in collecting the data that you need.

▶ Some advice

When you discuss your proposed outline research design with your supervisor, it is likely that he or she will offer some advice. Your supervisor might, for example, suggest some modification such as the deletion of a variable or the addition of a new variable, or perhaps that you should truncate your design in some way. Whether or not you take such advice is *your* decision. However, you should bear in mind that your supervisor has had personal experience in research, and would have supervised other students in the past. Moreover, remember that your supervisor will want to help you. The advice offered, therefore, will be based on experience and will be well intentioned. You would, then, do well to consider seriously any advice that your supervisor offers.

5 Detailed Design and Planning

Having designed your research in outline, you need to design it in detail and to plan its execution. It is important to do this carefully because so much detail is involved; it is very easy to miss something. For instance, although suitable participants might be available, it is easy to overlook the possibility that they might not be so when you need them. An example of such an oversight is provided by a student who went on a field trip during which she intended to gather data. After she arrived at her destination, she discovered that she had forgotten to obtain a particular test that she needed. This caused her some considerable inconvenience.

When designing and planning your research, it is advisable to prepare a list of the necessary tasks so that you do not overlook anything. The tasks involved will vary with the nature of your research, but the following list should cover most situations.

1. Design in detail an experiment or study to investigate the research question, and decide on suitable techniques for analysis of the data.
2. If an external organization is involved, obtain necessary approval.
3. Ensure that suitable participants, respondents, or subjects are available.
4. Arrange availability of any apparatus or materials needed.
5. Estimate the time needed for collection of the necessary data.
6. Prepare a research proposal.
7. Make any necessary changes to the research design.
8. Obtain ethics approval.
9. Arrange availability of laboratory space or a room for testing.
10. Arrange availability of participants, respondents, or subjects.

You should list the necessary tasks in a logical sequence such as that shown above. However, it is important to understand that aspects of any one task are likely to affect one or more other tasks. For example, the design of an experiment and the nature of any apparatus that you intend to use involve interrelated considerations. In some instances, a problem that arises in one task might result in the completion of another being impossible. As an example, although suitable participants might be available through an external organization, that organization might not grant approval for your research. Although, then, you should complete the necessary tasks in a logical and progressive sequence, when working on a given task you must always consider any possible effects arising out of any other task(s).

▶ Research design and data analysis

You will already be familiar with research design and data analysis. However, especially if you have not previously designed a research project, you might find the following notes useful.

Perhaps, the most important point to emphasize is that the research design and intended data analysis are intimately interrelated. Designing the research and selecting a suitable approach to data analysis, therefore, must be carried out concurrently. On occasion, students overlook this critical point and they do not plan the analysis of data when designing their research. The result can be that, having collected their data, they encounter serious problems with the necessary analysis.

Research design

Research must be designed to find a solution or partial solution to the research problem being addressed. More specifically, it must be designed to find an answer to the research question that is being investigated. Although this might seem to be such an obvious point as not to warrant a mention, it is surprising how often students have to be reminded of it. There seems to be a tendency for students to lose sight of the aim of their research while they are involved in the details of its design.

Finding the answer to a research question always requires measuring some variable(s) and, if a causal relationship is being investigated, manipulating some variable(s). It follows that the first step in designing a piece of research is to define the variables involved – where necessary, in operational terms. The second step is to select or devise a method for measuring the variables involved. If manipulation of a variable is required, a method of doing so must also be devised. These are critical considerations because the design of any piece of research is limited by what is possible. There must be some valid method of measuring the variables involved. In addition, if the research is designed to investigate a causal relationship, there must be some method of effectively manipulating the independent variable(s).

When designing your research, you should not overlook the expected or desired strength of effect. In addition, you should consider the power of your research design.

Pilot research

It is always a good idea to carry out pilot research. Doing so allows for detecting any unforeseen problems. For instance, some problem with apparatus might be found, a flaw in a questionnaire might become apparent, or participants might experience undue difficulty with performing some experimental task. Any problems such as these will need to be rectified before beginning the research proper.

When pilot research is carried out simply as a "test run", no particular planning is involved, other than to allow time and make arrangements for carrying it out. If no problem becomes apparent the pilot research effectively becomes part of the data collection for the research proper, and no distinction need be made.

On the other hand, pilot research is sometimes carried out for a specific purpose. This might be, for example, to test some piece of apparatus, to confirm that the manipulation of some variable is effective, or to allow for an estimate of the strength of effect of some manipulation. In this case, the pilot research is separate from the research proper, and must be planned as such. Effectively, the research project becomes one involving two (or more) experiments or studies, and participants, respondents, or subjects involved in the pilot research must be excluded from the subsequent data collection proper.

An important consideration is that if, as a result of pilot research, any material change to the original research design becomes necessary, this must be approved by the university ethics committee, and by any external ethics committee involved, before data collection for the research proper can begin. When planning time for carrying out the research, therefore, allowance for this eventuality must be made.

Validation research

When validation research is involved this must be planned as an integral part of the research project. Although it may be regarded in a sense as being separate from the research proper, the same considerations are involved in both. In this case, the validation research is designed to validate some instrument that is to be used in the research. Validation research, therefore, must be completed – including analysis and interpretation of the data collected – before the research proper can begin.

If any material changes are made to the research design as a result of the outcome of validation research, these must be approved by the university ethics committee, and by any external ethics committee involved, before continuing. This is so regardless of whether further validation research is required or the research proper is to begin.

Participants, respondents, or subjects involved in the validation research must be excluded from the research proper.

Ethics
You will no doubt, and in any event you must, consider ethical issues when designing your research. Ethical issues are discussed in Chapter 6, and you would be well advised to read this chapter before you design your research.

Data recording
You need to consider how you intend to record the data that you collect. In the case of survey research, the raw data will often be in the form of written responses to questionnaires, and in qualitative research in the form of interview notes, or perhaps audio recordings that will be transcribed. For other forms of research, raw data will typically be in numerical form, recorded either in writing or electronically. Whatever the form, you need to decide how you will record and securely store your data.

In any event, you will no doubt enter the raw data into a computer file for purposes of analysis. You would be well advised to do this as you progress with data collection, and you should keep a back-up copy of this file in another location. Although perhaps unlikely, mishaps such as fire and flood do arise, and computer "crashes" are not uncommon. If any such event were to occur – and you do not have a back-up – you could lose your data, which would present a rather serious problem.

On one occasion, a student placed the file containing her hand-written data on the roof of her car while she searched her pockets for her car keys. Having found her keys, she got into her car and drove away. Only later, when she looked for her data file, did she recall putting it on the roof of her car. She returned to the scene and searched for her lost data but, not surprisingly, she did not find the file. The problem was that she had not made a back-up copy.

Data analysis

The data analysis technique(s) to be used must "fit with" the research design. Again, this might seem to a point that is so obvious that it need not be mentioned, but it is surprising how often it is overlooked. This applies equally to data analysis techniques used in both quantitative and qualitative research, but problems are more commonly encountered in the former.

Perhaps because of lack of confidence in their knowledge of statistics, students sometimes seem to be fixated on the use of some particular technique for data analysis – whether or not it is appropriate to their particular research design. On the other hand, sometimes they design their research to suit a data analysis technique with which they are familiar, which can result in a poor, or at least not optimal, research design.

When the research is of a quantitative nature, data analyses will involve testing for some relationship between variables – usually of a causal nature. Typically, this will require the testing of hypotheses, and so the analysis selected must allow for this. In some instances, preliminary analyses and perhaps some form of data transformation might be required. You should consider such a possibility.

Analyses of data collected in qualitative research will also involve investigating some relationship(s) between variables. In this case, it is unlikely that the relationships will be of a causal nature, and the testing of explicit hypotheses might not be involved. It remains, however, that you must select some suitable approach to data analysis that has at least the potential to provide an answer to your research question.

Hypotheses

Commonly, investigating a research question will involve the developing and testing of hypotheses. When this is so, the intended research must be designed to test them effectively. You will already be familiar with the development of hypotheses, but it might be of value to make some comments here.

A particular point, which is often overlooked, is that there is a difference between theoretical and research (or experimental) hypotheses. Obviously, a theoretical hypothesis is developed on the basis of some theory, and proposes some relationship between two or more concepts or constructs. A research hypothesis, on the other hand, is in the form of a predicted relationship between the variables involved in the research. The former, therefore, is theory-dependent whereas the latter is research design-dependent.

It is important to understand that developing theoretical hypotheses is not simply a matter of proposing some relationship between two or more concepts or constructs. The proposed relationship must be such that supporting it will potentially provide a solution or partial solution to the research problem being addressed. Similarly, it is important to understand that developing research hypotheses is not simply a matter of predicting some expected outcome of a piece of research. Rather, research hypotheses must be such that supporting them will provide an answer to the research question being investigated.

Numerous research hypotheses can be developed from a single theoretical hypothesis, and students sometimes develop a large number that they intend to test. It is important to understand that hypotheses are useful only in so far that testing of them will potentially provide an answer to the specific research question being investigated. Therefore, it follows that only those that are necessary should be tested. In any event, it is usually not advisable to test a large number of hypotheses. Doing so often merely adds unnecessary complexity to the research. It is, therefore, preferable to concentrate on a limited number – perhaps only one. On the other hand, the number of hypotheses necessary to provide an answer to the research question being investigated must be tested.

Research hypotheses

When planning your research you will develop the hypotheses that you intend to test, but it is not adequate simply to "know" what they are. You must write them, and it is critical to ensure that research hypotheses are concisely and clearly expressed. For example, the following hypothesis proposed by one student is overly long and is difficult to understand.

> The majority of respondents, aged between 35 and 55 years who are in full-time paid employment and are classified as being in a managerial or professional occupation group, who work 45 or more hours per week, will report being less satisfied with their lives compared to the majority of other white collar occupation group respondents who work less than 45 hours per week, who are in full time employment and are aged between 35 and 55 years.

Clearly, the research involved is intended to investigate satisfaction with life of "white collar" workers who are in full-time paid employment in a managerial or professional occupation, and who are between 35 and 55 years of age. There must be some reason for selecting this particular group; and, when the introduction is written, this must be made clear, and the meaning of "white collar" workers should be operationally defined. In addition, there must be some reason for comparing the two age groups, and again this must be made clear in the introduction. Finally, the groups working longer or shorter hours must be defined in operational terms in the introduction. For example, they could be defined as those working longer and those working shorter hours, with appropriate hours of work given. The hypothesis, then, could have been worded as

> The majority of those working longer hours will report less satisfaction with life than will those working shorter hours.

This is a much shorter and simpler hypothesis, which is much more easily understood. However, there are still problems with it. Presumably some instrument, such as the Life Satisfaction Scale, will be used to measure the participants' satisfaction with life – and this must be discussed in detail in the introduction. In addition, while it is possible to hypothesize that "the majority of a group will ...", it is more likely that a comparison will be made between mean scores. Therefore, the hypothesis could be rewritten as

> The mean life satisfaction score of the longer-working-hours group will be lower than that of the shorter-working-hours group.

The rewritten hypothesis is in the form of a single, clear, declarative sentence – and uses terms that previously have been operationally defined. Notice that there is no reference to "white collar" workers, their ages, or to them being in full-time paid employment. This is not necessary, because only those who fit within the defined group will be included in the research.

This might seem to have been an unduly long discussion of research hypotheses. However, it is important to understand that quantitative research revolves around the hypotheses involved. In particular, the research will be designed to test a research hypothesis (or perhaps more than one) and so indirectly the theoretical hypothesis. Writing research hypotheses clearly and simply defines exactly what you expect to find in your research. Moreover, doing so allows you to ensure that your research design can effectively test the hypothesis or hypotheses involved.

Qualitative research

In qualitative research, it may be that explicit hypotheses are not tested. On the other hand, based on previous research and/or logical reasoning, it is often possible to make some prediction with regard to the outcome. Although not a hypothesis in the conventional sense, such a prediction can give direction to research and suggest how the expected outcome might provide an answer to the research question. Clearly, this is an essential consideration when designing a piece of research. Where possible, therefore, you should develop any such predication in a manner similar to that used when developing hypotheses.

External organization involvement

If the involvement of an external organization is necessary for you to carry out your intended research, you will already have considered this. In particular, you should have approached the organization and gained at least "in-principle" approval. There would be no point in planning your research in detail if you had not done so.

You should also have obtained from the organization details of the requirements for granting of approval for your research. At this point, therefore, you need to plan how and when you are to comply with these requirements. You will also need to arrange to have access to participants, respondents, or subjects at an appropriate time. In addition, you need to make any other necessary arrangements, such as availability of a room in which to carry out your research.

Ethics

Apart from any other requirements, some organizations have an ethics committee and, when this is so, you will have to apply to that committee for ethics approval – in addition to the relevant university ethics committee.

Initially, you might find that you can only be given approval "in principle". This is likely because, at the beginning, you will not have designed your research in detail and so cannot give the organization all of the information that is required. There is a risk associated with such in-principle approval: Final approval might not be granted.

Time

When planning your research you will have to consider the time that will be needed to gain approval from any external organization involved. If the organization has its own ethics committee, this will be at least partly determined by the dates on which it meets. A point to note is that you can expect that you will not be able to apply for ethics approval from your university until approval has been granted by the external organization. In addition, you should bear in mind that the external organization and/or the university ethics committee might require changes to your research design before granting final approval, which can result in a delay in beginning data collection.

Participants, respondents, or subjects

You will already have considered the availability of participants, respondents, or subjects when examining the feasibility of your intended research. At this point, therefore, you should only need to arrange to have access to them when needed.

If your research involves preliminary testing to identify suitable participants, respondents, or subjects, you will also already have considered this. In particular, you should have decided on what testing is required and how you intend to carry this out. Therefore, you should at this point only need to plan the necessary arrangements.

Number

When your intended research is of an experimental nature and involves multiple conditions, you will need to estimate the number of participants or subjects needed in each condition. In particular, if the research is multifactorial you will need to estimate the number needed in each cell.

Similar considerations are involved in survey research. An adequate number of respondents is needed for valid statistical analyses. This can sometimes present a problem even when a simple comparison between groups is required. The problem can be exacerbated in the case of multifactorial research because, for analyses to be valid, the numbers involved in groups and cells will need to be at least similar. Therefore, you need to be reasonably confident that you can achieve this.

In qualitative research the numbers needed are difficult to estimate. How many people have to be involved will vary with the specific nature of the research and the intended form of data analyses. In any event, at least a substantial number of people will be needed, and some reasonably accurate estimate of numbers is necessary.

Apparatus and materials

When examining the feasibility of your research, you will have considered the availability of any necessary apparatus or materials. Regardless of the nature of resources that you need for your research, you must arrange for them to be available when needed. This means that you will have to take into consideration any time involved, such as that needed to obtain, or design and develop, the required resources.

Time needed for data collection

You need to make a reasonably accurate estimate of the time that will be needed to collect data – including that needed for any pilot research. This is necessary so that you can plan your time and that you can ensure that any necessary apparatus or material, participants, respondents, or subjects, and, when needed, a laboratory or room for testing are available.

In the case of experimental research, this is relatively straightforward, and will usually involve simply calculating the time needed to test the necessary number of participants in the conditions in your experiment (including practice trials). However, there can be a difference between the time required to complete a task, and the time by which you can have it completed. For example, collecting data might require 60 hours of testing, which you might equate to, say, 12 days' work. On the other hand, because you will have to fit this in with your other commitments and with the availability of participants, data collection might, for instance, involve 6 weeks (i.e., 2 days per week).

When research involves participants or respondents in completing some instrument, such as a questionnaire or personality inventory on a "face-to-face" basis, similar calculations can be made. However, if the instrument is to be distributed by mail and returned by the same means, the time required to collect data is more difficult to estimate. In this case, you will have to allow time for mail delivery and for respondents to complete and return the instrument. Then, you will have to set some "cut-off" date. Not all instruments will be returned, and you cannot simply wait and hope that more will arrive.

In the case of qualitative research, estimating the time needed to collect the necessary data can be problematic. For instance, it can be difficult to estimate the time needed to complete an interview, and the availability of participants can make it difficult to plan time. Moreover, because the research design can be modified in unforeseen ways during the collection of data, it can be impossible to predict with any accuracy the time that might be involved. Nonetheless, some estimate of the time needed to collect data must be made. In some instances, this might necessitate simply allotting a period of time to the collection of data.

Research proposal

When you have completed its design and planning, you need to make a final evaluation of your intended research. Because you will have designed and planned it over some time, there is always the possibility that something has been overlooked. This is particularly so because you will no doubt have changed some of your initial ideas as a result of discussing them with your supervisor (and no doubt others), and you will probably have made changes to parts of your proposed research as you progressed with your planning. It is, therefore, important to review your intended research in its entirety before you begin to collect data. In particular, you need to ensure that the parts of your design and plan "fit together", and that you detect any potential problems.

Once you have finalized your research design and your plan for its execution, you need to present these to your supervisor so that he or she can evaluate them. It may be that all that is expected of you is to present your ideas and your research design to your supervisor verbally, although no doubt with the support of some pre-prepared illustrations such as diagrams of the layout of apparatus or a graph of the expected pattern of results. More commonly, however, you will be expected to submit a written research proposal to your supervisor.

Like you, your supervisor will have considered your intended research in parts as you discussed each with him or her, but this will have occurred over a lengthy period. During this time, the academic involved will have devoted his or her attention to a range of activities, and, no doubt, will have discussed research with other students. It is, therefore, unlikely that your supervisor will readily be able to bring to mind a complete and detailed account of your intended research. Before discussing your proposed research in its entirety, therefore, you should give a written research proposal to your supervisor. This will allow him or her to review your proposed research as a whole, and the time necessary to think about it before discussing it with you.

In any event, the most effective way for you to review your proposed research is to write a research proposal. Because writing is a discipline that leads to analytical, critical, and logical thinking, this forces you to consider carefully each aspect of your proposed research. Such careful consideration should ensure that you do not encounter any unexpected problems after you have begun to collect data, when you subsequently analyse the data collected, and when you write your thesis.

Requirement

A programme of study may require that students submit a written research proposal. Some, in addition, require that students present their research proposals to a committee of academics or at a seminar attended by academics and fellow students. Details of any such requirement will be provided to students, typically in a handbook for the programme given to them. In any event, you need to understand that the preparation and writing of a research proposal and the preparation for a research proposal seminar requires considerable time and effort. (Preparing and writing a research proposal is discussed in Chapter 7, and presenting a research proposal seminar is discussed in Chapter 8.)

Changes to your research design

As a result of discussing your research proposal with your supervisor, and if required having written a research proposal and possibly presented a research proposal seminar, you are likely to find that some changes to your intended research are advisable. You should carefully consider any suggestions that have been made or any advice offered, and make any changes to your research that you think are necessary.

Ethics approval

When you have finalized the design of your intended research, you will have to gain ethics approval from the university ethics committee before you can begin to collect data. (Ethical issues are discussed in Chapter 6.) You will have been given the necessary details, most likely in the handbook for the programme of study given to you. All that you need to do now is to comply with the necessary requirements.

Similarly, if an external organization is involved, you might have to submit an ethics application to its ethics committee. Again, what is required will vary between organizations, and you will have to ascertain and comply with the requirements involved.

Gaining ethics approval is *your* responsibility, not your supervisor's. In particular, it is your responsibility to complete the necessary documentation, submit the ethics application, and provide the ethics committee with any additional information required. If necessary, you will have to make any required changes to the research design and submit an amended ethics application.

Ensuring that you gain ethics approval is critical. On one occasion, an honours student believed that she had been granted ethics approval by a correctional establishment for access to inmates, but this had been granted only in principle, and was later withdrawn. As a result, she was unable to complete her honours degree until the following year. Fortunately, under those circumstances, the university allowed her to re-enrol. Nonetheless, it required a further year for her to complete her studies.

Availability of laboratory space, or a room, for testing

Typically, research projects require participants to perform some task. For instance, this might involve the use of apparatus, entering information into a computer, a pencil and paper task, or participating in an interview. Whatever the task, it has to be performed somewhere. It is important to ensure the availability of laboratory space or a suitable room for testing or interviewing.

When apparatus or a computer is involved, the research is likely to be carried out in a laboratory or some similar environment. On the other hand, if the task is of a pencil and paper nature or an interview, it is likely that all that is required is a quiet, distraction-free room. In any event, consideration has to be given to the availability of laboratory space or a suitable room. Usually, if arrangements are made early, there will be suitable facilities available in the department.

A problem can often arise, however, if research has to be conducted elsewhere. For instance, children might have to be tested at school. In other instances, the research might, for example, involve interviewing participants or respondents at their place of work, in a hospital, or at home. In such circumstances, it is often difficult to find a suitable place in which to carry out the research. Nonetheless, this has to be catered for when planning your project.

Availability of participants, respondents, or subjects

You will have considered the availability of participants, respondents, or subjects when designing your research in outline. At this point, you need to make the necessary arrangements for them to be available at the required time and place, which will require appropriate negotiation.

▶ Research involving multiple experiments or studies

Planning a research project that includes multiple experiments or studies requires essentially the same procedures as for one in which only a single experiment or study is involved. The obvious difference is that some of the planning steps must be repeated for each. However, because the outcome of the first experiment or study must lead logically to the next, it is difficult to plan ahead in detail. Consequently, some conjecture will be involved, and some aspects can only be planned in detail after the preceding experiment or study has been completed, and the outcome interpreted.

▶ Group research projects

Departments vary in their requirements for group research projects and in their associated policies; but, in general, the advice that has been offered here with regard to preparation and planning of an individual research project is, with minor modification, equally applicable to a group research project. There are, however, some particular points that should be made in relation to group research projects.

Research design and data analysis

Largely, as a result of the research problem to be investigated being given, it is probable that the outline research design has been essentially predetermined – but usually only in general terms. You can expect, then, that you will be involved in designing the research in detail. A point in this regard that you need to understand is that, because of required differences in students' theses, the research design will probably involve some relatively minor inclusions to suit variations in individual students' work. Such an inclusion might, for example, be the addition of some variable to allow an individual student to test a particular hypothesis.

It is most likely that the group will be responsible for selection of appropriate techniques for data analysis. In addition, where students are investigating individual research questions and/or testing individual research hypotheses, perhaps in addition to some common one, the individual student involved will be responsible for selection of appropriate techniques for analysis of the relevant data.

Planning the research

Although restricted in some areas, you can expect that the group will have to plan the research in detail in the same way as would students who are working on an individual research project.

Allotting tasks

An aspect of planning a group research project that is not applicable to individual research projects is the allotting of tasks. It is likely that some tasks will be allotted to individuals on the basis of a group decision, but the group as a whole has to be satisfied with the outcome. Individual members of the group are obligated to carry out any such tasks satisfactorily and by the target date set.

Research proposal

It is unlikely that a group research proposal will be required for a group research project. However, it is quite possible that individual research proposals will be. These may be verbal or written, depending on the programme requirements and department policy. Such requirements will usually be included in a handbook for the programme of study.

Ethics approval

A group research project is a single project. Therefore, a single ethics application is needed by the university ethics committee, and by any external ethics committee that might be involved. This application must describe the research design, including variations that are included to cater for any individual student's requirements.

Gaining ethics approval is a *group responsibility*, not the supervisor's. In particular, it is the group's responsibility to complete the necessary documentation, submit the ethics application, provide the ethics committee with any additional information required, and, if necessary, make any required changes to the research design and submit an amended ethics application.

While preparation of the ethics application is a group responsibility, and all group members must sign it, usually one student will have to be nominated as the "principal investigator" for purposes of submitting the application and responding to any correspondence from the ethics committee(s). It is this student's responsibility to submit the ethics application, to keep other group members informed, to provide the committee with any additional information required, to arrange with the group any necessary changes to the research design, and, if necessary, to submit an amended ethics application.

Data collection

Data collection will be shared among the group, and how this is to be achieved will have to be decided by the group on some appropriate basis. Similarly, entering data into a common computer file will be a group responsibility. Therefore, matters such as the format of the data file must be decided on a group basis.

It can be expected that it will be necessary to collect data from at least two groups and perhaps two or more sub-groups in any research project. Obviously, then, data from the groups and any sub-groups involved must be available when needed for the necessary analysis. Data collection, therefore, should be shared among members of the group so that in the event of any student failing to collect data by the target date set for completion of this task, the remaining group members can still carry out an appropriate and valid data analysis.

A point to note is that, if any student fails to complete data collection by the agreed target date but subsequently does so, it is highly unlikely that the other group members would allow their data to be used by that group member. Doing so would result in that student having a larger sample size in the groups and perhaps sub-groups involved, and so possibly a more valid analysis. The result could be that other group members are disadvantaged. Conversely, a student who is not allowed to use other group members' data will be disadvantaged.

Time plan

A group time plan must be prepared. This is a particularly important aspect of the planning of group research project. With the exception of the due date for individual research proposals if required, that for submission of the theses, and any other specific deadlines given, target dates for completion of tasks must be set by the group.

A problem can arise if a target date is not achieved. This can result in some students not being able to progress satisfactorily with their individual work, which can cause considerable friction. The setting of target dates for completion of tasks, therefore, should be regarded as a "group contract", and all group members must fulfil their obligations under this contract.

Meetings

Apart from planning time for the research, the group needs to arrange times for regular meetings. It is also a good idea to keep minutes of meetings and to distribute them to all members of the group after a meeting. Such minutes need not be particularly formal, but they need to include any group decisions such as allocation of tasks and target dates set. Doing this can prevent later disagreement and any resulting friction.

In addition to these group meetings, there will also be a need to arrange frequent and regular meetings with the group's supervisor(s). It is likely that some such meetings will be held on a group basis, while others will be held with individual students. As a group, or where appropriate as an individual, you will need to make appropriate arrangements with your supervisor(s).

Progress

A final point that it is necessary to understand is that it is the *group*'s responsibility to ensure that satisfactory progress is made. Similarly, it is the responsibility of *individual members* of the group to ensure that they maintain satisfactory progress with any aspect of the research that is peculiar to them – in particular, any necessary individual variations on the group research design.

Withdrawal

If any member of the group withdraws from his or her study, he or she is obliged to inform other group members immediately. Failure to do so can result in other students wasting time trying to contact the "missing member". More importantly, if some task has been allotted to that individual and this has not been completed, other group members must know that the student has withdrawn so that alternative arrangements can be made.

▶ Problems

No doubt, you will encounter some problems with the designing and planning of your research. As an individual, or as a group, you should initially try to solve any problem that you encounter. If you find a solution, you will derive a great deal of satisfaction from your achievement. On the other hand, there is no need to be overly independent. Your supervisor will be more than willing to offer you advice and guidance. (Problems and the taking of advice are discussed in Chapter 3.)

You should understand that you are not expected to be able to design and plan a piece of research with complete independence, either as an individual or as a group. Rather, you are developing your existing research skills and abilities. It follows that you are free to ask for help when needed. Supervisors will always be willing to offer advice and guidance, and more so if the student(s) involved has (have) made some attempt to solve the problem encountered before asking for help.

6 Ethics

Those who carry out research have a moral obligation to ensure that what they do does not detrimentally affect anyone. Unfortunately, in the past this has not always been recognized, and some research that has been carried out has been at least questionable. Attention was particularly drawn to this by reports of research carried out by some German scientists during the Second World War, in which people were inhumanely treated. As a result, various bodies, such as the Australian and British Psychological Societies, and the American Psychological Association produced ethical guidelines for their members. These principles cover all psychological practice, including research. Similarly, other organizations such as universities and hospitals have developed ethical guidelines.

Although you will be given detailed requirements and directed to appropriate documents, difficulties can sometimes arise as a result of a lack of understanding of the principles involved, or because the documentation to which you have been referred does not provide a solution to some particular problem with which you are faced. Because the nature of research varies widely, no documentation can cater for every eventuality. Therefore, the following overview of ethics requirements and some advice are offered to help you to avoid potential difficulties when designing and planning your research.

▶ Approval

Before any research involving humans or animals may be carried out by staff or students of a university, it must be approved of by an ethics committee. Universities vary in how they deal with this need. In some, all applications for ethics approval are considered by a single committee, while in others the task is shared among faculty or department committees.

Many other organizations also require ethics approval for research. When this is so, before research can be carried out within that organization, it must be approved of by its ethics committee. Before carrying out research that involves an external organization that has an ethics committee, therefore, staff or students of a university must gain ethics approval from both the university's and the organization's ethics committees.

It is possible that an ethics committee will not approve of proposed research, or will do so only if the research design is modified in some way. Usually, however, ethical requirements do not present any difficulties if they have been considered when planning the research, and the necessary documentation has been adequately and correctly prepared.

You will be given details of the requirements of the appropriate ethics committee in your university; but if your research involves an external organization, you will have to ascertain that organization's requirements. Commonly, you will be directed to one or more documents such as the university's or organization's policy on ethics, and often the ethical requirements of other bodies. In any event, you will be required to document your application for ethics approval – typically by completing an application form and attaching any additional documents required.

▶ Modifications

Sometimes, an ethics committee will require some modification to proposed research or to documents, such as an information letter or consent form, or request additional information. Usually, this means that the ethics application has to be resubmitted, and that the revised application will be considered by the committee at its next meeting. If the committee meets infrequently, the resultant delay can present a major problem for the student. Data collection may not begin until ethics approval has been granted, and students have limited time in which to complete a research project.

▶ Considerations

When examining proposed research, an ethics committee will primarily be concerned with any possibility of what might be described as "harm" to participants or respondents – either directly or indirectly. In this context, harm has a wide meaning. It includes any possible physical or psychological harm (including discomfort or embarrassment), or the possibility of damage to the interests or reputations of those involved.

Apart from any possible effects on participants or respondents, in some instances there are more general considerations. For instance, the research might involve some minority group in the population such as people of a particular religious or sexual persuasion, or a particular cultural or ethnic group. When this is so, the committee will consider any possible effects on the group. As an example, a particular group of indigenous people might have what are regarded as "secret sacred rituals". Although some members of the group who are directly involved in the research might be willing to divulge information about these rituals, others might consider such a revelation to be severely detrimental to their religion or culture. Australian Aborigines, for instance, are particularly sensitive in regard to secret rituals and rites.

The ethics committee will need to be satisfied that the people who are involved are fully informed regarding the nature of the research and any possible effects on them. People must always give their fully informed consent before participating in any research.

In addition, the committee will need to be satisfied that those participating will do so on a completely voluntary basis (i.e., there must be no direct or indirect inducement or coercion). This can be a contentious issue. For example, students are sometimes expected to participate in research as part of course requirements. Also, people are sometimes paid for participation in research. Organizations can have differing policies on such matters.

Finally, the committee will need to be satisfied that appropriate steps are to be taken to ensure that anonymity of individuals and confidentiality of data collected are maintained.

There will be specific requirements if any medical procedures are involved. Similarly, when research involves animals there will be requirements with regard to issues such as care, handling, and disposal. In such circumstances, the requirements of the university and any external organization involved will have to be determined.

▶ Requirements

The basic requirements with regard to human participants are generally common. These are informed consent, voluntary participation, freedom to withdraw at any time, and confidentiality. To ensure that these requirements are met, ethics committees typically require a procedure of explanation and documentation.

Explanation

As a first requirement, the nature and purpose of the research, and any possible effects (including any possible after-effects that they might experience) must be clearly explained to those who are asked to participate. If the research involves an investigation of some problems that individuals experience or disorders from which they suffer, they must also be advised that the research will not directly provide an answer to their problems or a cure for their disorders.

Having explained the nature of the research, prospective participants must be assured that their identities will not be revealed, either directly or indirectly. In addition, they must be assured that the raw data collected will be treated as being confidential; that it will be securely stored; and that it will be destroyed on completion of the research or at some other specified time.

In the case of survey research, or any research involving responding to questions, those who are asked to participate should be advised that they are not compelled to answer any particular question if they do not wish to do so.

Finally, and most importantly, those approached must be assured that their participation is entirely voluntary and that they are free to withdraw from the research at any time. In some instances, it will also be necessary to ensure individuals that refusal to participate or subsequent withdrawal from the research will not have a particular effect on them. As an example, if the participants were patients in a hospital, it would be necessary to assure them that refusal to participate in the research would have no effect on their treatment.

Information letter

To ensure that prospective participants are fully informed and are aware of their rights, ethics committees usually insist that – in addition to a verbal explanation – the nature and purpose of the research and the rights of those involved are explained to them in writing. This is done in what is usually described as an *information letter* (or perhaps an information sheet). There is no particular format for an information letter, but it must include specific information.

Usually, the information letter is headed with the name of the research project. It then begins by explaining that the research is being carried out as part of the student's study, and gives the student's name. In addition, the name and contact details of the student's supervisor are given so that, if they wish, participants can contact him or her.

The verbal explanation given to participants is then given in writing, followed by a statement that the research has been approved by the appropriate ethics committee of the university. If an external organization is involved, a statement to the effect that this organization also has approved the research must be included. The name and contact details of a representative of the university ethics committee, who may be contacted by the participant in the event that he or she has any concerns about the research, must be included.

This information letter must be given to and be retained by each participant.

Consent form

The ethics committee will usually insist that participants sign a consent form and that the signed form be retained by the investigator. Institutions will have their own specific requirements for the form and content of consent forms. In principle, however, consent forms will be similar to the example given in Box 1.

Box 1   An example consent form

Rapid Response Research Project
being carried out by Mr I.M. Tardy under the supervision of
Dr B.E. Quik

I .... have been fully informed of the purpose and nature of this research project, and I have read the information letter provided to me. I understand that my participation is completely voluntary, and that I am free to withdraw at any time.

Signature .... Date......................

▶ Children

When the participants in research are children, the same verbal explanation given to prospective adult participants should be given to the child's parent(s) or guardian. In any event, a parent or guardian must read the information letter and sign the consent form. Only a parent's or a guardian's consent is required for children to participate in research. However, although of no legal effect, it is advisable to ask older children to sign the consent form in addition to the parent or guardian.

Regardless of a parent's or a guardian's consent, the research must be explained to children (in language that they can be expected to understand) and they must agree to participate. Children may not be coerced into participation, or into continuing to participate, if they wish to withdraw from the research.

▶ Schools

If children are to be involved in research at a school, approval of the school must be obtained. This will require consent from the principal, and often from class teachers. In addition, in the case of government schools, approval from the education department might be needed. Similarly, in the case of private schools, it might be that the school board must give approval.

Having gained approval from the school and any other approval required, it remains that parents or guardians – and the children themselves – must consent to participate in the research. It is usually impossible to give a verbal explanation of the research to parents or guardians. Therefore, consent is commonly obtained from parents or guardians by "sending home" with children the information letter and the consent form.

▶ Infants

Particularly careful consideration must be given to ethical issues when research involves infants. Obviously, they cannot understand what is happening to them, and cannot communicate their feelings, other than by crying or some physical response. It is, therefore, particularly important to explain very clearly to infants' parents what is involved, and to ensure that they give fully informed consent for the infant's participation in the research. With very rare exception, one of the infants' parents must be present during the data collection. If an infant appears to be distressed, the data collection must be discontinued immediately.

▶ Individuals who are unable to give informed consent

In some instances, prospective participants in research cannot give informed consent. The research might, for example, be designed to investigate some aspect of a disorder that renders those affected incapable of sufficient understanding of what is involved. When this is so, consent for the individuals involved to participate in the research must be obtained from their guardians. Even when this permission is given, the investigator still has a responsibility to ensure that no "harm" is caused to participants in the course of the research.

▶ Special groups

Careful consideration must be given to the involvement of individuals from special groups such as members of the armed services or employees of some organization. The considerations for such groups will differ, and so it is impossible to be specific. However, it is important to ensure that the rights of individuals are not put in jeopardy. In particular, it is essential to ensure that participation is voluntary (i.e., there is no coercion to participate) and that strict confidentiality is maintained.

▶ Photographic or audio recording

In some research, it might be necessary to make a photographic record of participants. An example is the video recording of children's behaviour. In other research, it might be necessary, or convenient, to make an audio recording. An example of this is the recording of interviews that will subsequently be transcribed. If there is any relevant legislation that includes specific requirements relating to such recordings, it will be necessary to comply with this.

In any event, when photographic and/or audio recordings are to be made, fully informed consent of participants to do so must be obtained. This will involve explaining the reason for making the recording, for what purpose it will be used, who will have access to it, how confidentiality of the recording is to be assured, for how long it will be kept, and details of its subsequent disposal.

As for any other aspect of the research, explanations regarding the making of recordings must be given to participants both verbally and in the written information letter that is given to them. In addition, consent to make such recordings must be included in the signed consent form.

▶ Confidentiality

The identity of those who participate in research must not be revealed either directly or indirectly. If it is necessary to refer to an individual participant when reporting the research, this may be done by the use of initials (possibly fictitious) or a number (e.g., Participant 5). In addition, other information that is gathered during the course of the research must be protected. For instance, it might be necessary to gather information from material that is confidential. As an example, a research project might be designed to investigate the interpretation of some test (e.g., a personality inventory) in psychological reports. Gaining approval for access to such material can sometimes present ethical problems.

As an example of a potential problem, if a psychologist carries out a psychological assessment of an individual, the report that is written is confidential. It might be that such a report is held in, for instance, the hospital records of a patient. However, the hospital cannot grant access to that report without the consent of the patient. In some circumstances, the consent of the psychologist who wrote the report might also be necessary.

Information in other forms can also be sensitive. As an example, before beginning research that involves an investigation of minority, ethnic, religious, or indigenous groups, consultation with the leaders of such groups is required. For instance, it is likely that, before beginning research involving an indigenous group, approval from tribal elders might be needed. Even then, the research might well result in dissension within the group, and unforeseen problems can arise. It might be, for instance, that there can be different interpretations of the outcome, and not all might be considered favourably by some members of the group. As another example, it might be that some implication of the outcome is not looked upon favourably by some.

▶ Deception

Most people are not only co-operative but will try to help an investigator by producing the desired results. Often, therefore, it is necessary to deceive participants. Typically, such deception is quite innocuous. Nonetheless, deception can be a contentious issue. As a general principle, any deception involved in research should be explained to the participants, and justified, when data collection has been completed.

Such an explanation can sometimes pose a problem when the participants are drawn from some specific group if its members are in regular contact. A particular example is students, but other groups can pose similar problems. There is a possibility, especially if the research has to be carried out over a period of days or weeks, that those who have participated might reveal the deception to others who have not yet done so. How this problem is dealt with will vary. One option is simply to ask participants not to reveal the nature of the deception until the research has been completed. An alternative option is not to reveal the nature of the deception immediately after individuals have participated in the research, but to do so in a group debriefing when data collection has been completed.

▶ Debriefing

Participants must always be debriefed. They should be thanked for their participation, and the importance and potential value of the research should be emphasized. Put simply, they should be assured that their participation has been of value and that they have not wasted their time. In addition, participants should be given the opportunity to ask questions about the research. If a participant asks for a summary of the outcome of the research, it should be provided.

Often, participants are debriefed immediately after they have completed the required tasks. As an alternative, a group debriefing session may be arranged at a given time and place. In this case, participants should be thanked when the data have been collected, and advised of the time and place of the debriefing.

What is involved in the debriefing of children will vary with their age. Young children will have a limited capacity to understand the research, and so it might be that all that is possible is to thank them for their help. If a parent or guardian is present, he or she should be debriefed as would be an adult participant, and thanked for allowing the child to participate.

When research involves testing children at school, parents cannot readily be debriefed. One possibility is to arrange a debriefing session at the school and to send home with children a letter giving relevant details. Alternatively, it might be more appropriate to write a "debriefing letter" and to send this home with the children who participated. In any event, parents or guardians should, in some form, be thanked for allowing children to participate, and assured that their participation has been of value.

▶ Survey research

The ethical requirements of survey research are the same as those involved in other forms of research. There are, however, some aspects of informed consent and confidentiality that need to be considered. In particular, when questionnaires are distributed by mail or electronically online, it is obviously impossible to give a verbal explanation of the research, or for respondents to be verbally debriefed.

Information letter

As for other forms of research, respondents to a survey must be provided with an information letter that explains the nature of the research and includes all of the required information relating to it. When questionnaires are distributed by mail, the information letter must accompany them. If questionnaires are distributed electronically online, the information letter must be presented to respondents "on screen" before the questionnaire. In this case, the information letter should end with an instruction such as, "If you have read and understood the contents of this information letter and you are willing to proceed, press enter."

Consent

If questionnaires are returned by mail, it is not acceptable for the questionnaire and a signed consent form to be included in the same envelope, because doing so would reveal the respondent's identity. Therefore, it is usually acceptable to omit a signed consent form. In this case, the questionnaire must include a statement to the effect that by completing the questionnaire, the respondent has indicated voluntary consent to participation in the research. What is required is, in effect, a consent form – without name or signature – at the beginning of the questionnaire.

When questionnaires are distributed electronically online, it is, of course, impossible to provide a consent form. Therefore, the procedure described above should be adopted.

Confidentiality

Maintaining confidentiality in the case of survey research is usually straightforward. All that is required is that respondents' names must not appear on questionnaires. However, this can present a problem if it is necessary to identify individual respondents on some basis. For example, in research investigating attitude change, it might be necessary to relate responses in questionnaires administered on more than one occasion.

One approach to maintaining confidentiality in such a situation is to use a code of some form on questionnaires (e.g., identification numbers and/or letters), and to maintain a register of names and matching codes. In this case, the questionnaires and register must be stored separately and securely. Typically, this is done by storing them in separate locked filing cabinets to which only the investigator has a key.

On the other hand, respondents' names are not needed for this, and matching questionnaires using a code list is cumbersome. Therefore, it is preferable to give respondents instructions on how to devise an individual identification code on the first occasion, and ask them to write this on the questionnaire. For example, such a code could be devised using the last two letters of the first name of the respondent's mother and the day and month of her birth. The resulting code would be in the form of, for example, "th0207", and it would be highly unlikely that any two respondents would produce the same code. In addition, respondents can in future be reminded of how to devise the code. Using this technique, questionnaires can readily be related without recording respondents' names.

This procedure can also be followed when questionnaires are distributed electronically online. In this case, following the information letter, the necessary instructions can be presented "on screen" ending with, for example; "Please enter the code that you have devised in the box labelled 'ID Number' and press enter."

▶ Qualitative research

The ethical considerations that are relevant to other forms of research are equally relevant to qualitative research, but problems can sometimes arise in the latter. A particular problem can be maintaining confidentiality. Apart from the identities of the individuals, those of groups often must not be revealed. In some instances, members of a group might not be pleased if the name of the group was revealed in a research report. Similarly, a problem can arise when some specific geographic location, such as a small town, is involved in the research. Again, those who live in the location might not be pleased if its identity were to be revealed. Sometimes, it is possible to conceal or disguise the identity of groups or locations by use of initials or pseudonyms. Even when this is done, it might be that a description that is given of a particular group or geographical location could reveal its identity. For example, some years ago an investigation of the social structures in a small town in Australia was reported in a book. Although the author took pains to disguise the identity of the town, it had some unusual features and so could be identified by many people from its description.

▶ Potential problems

Typically, the research carried out by students is quite innocuous, and unlikely to have any harmful effects. Nonetheless, any possible effects must be considered. The potential problem is that, because of their lack of experience, students might not think of some possibility. This is particularly so, because students have limited time in which to carry out their research and they are usually very keen to start collecting data. It is, therefore, important to have their proposed research considered by others. The ethics committee fulfils this role.

Problems of an ethical nature in research can usually be avoided by careful thought in the planning stage, but unforeseen problems can sometimes present difficulties. Therefore, it is important to discuss ethical issues with your supervisor while designing a research project. Having begun your research, if any unforeseen problem arises, you should discuss it with your supervisor as soon as possible.

▶ A comment

Sometimes, students think that the requirement to gain ethics approval before they begin to collect data is simply a bureaucratic nuisance. It is important to understand that a consideration of ethical issues is a moral obligation. Anyone who is designing research must consider any possible effects on the participants, respondents, or subjects involved, and avoid anything that might cause "harm".

7 A Research Proposal

Put simply, a research proposal[1] is a document that describes a proposed piece of research in sufficient detail to allow for it to be evaluated. It begins with a literature review that identifies and defines the research problem, and defines the research question to be investigated. Following this, it describes the intended research and explains how the anticipated outcome is expected to provide a solution or partial solution to the research problem.

▶ Requirement

In some programmes of study, the research component is divided into two parts that are variously described as courses, subjects, modules, or units. In the first, students devise their research projects and write a research proposal, and in the second they carry out their research and write their theses. The aim of the first part is to prepare and plan a research project that is appropriate and workable, and to gain ethics approval for it. The aim of the second part is to carry out the research and write a satisfactory thesis.

Even if the research component of a programme is not divided in this manner, some departments still require the submission of a written research proposal. This is done to ensure that students are progressing satisfactorily, and that they have devised an appropriate and workable research project before they continue further.

▶ Time plan

Some departments require that a time plan in some form be submitted as part of a research proposal. Even if one is not required, you should prepare one. You need to do this to ensure (and to demonstrate) that you can complete your research and thesis within the time available. In addition, it will help you to monitor your progress.

Preparing such a time plan should be relatively straightforward. All that you need to do is to estimate the time needed to complete (or if necessary allot time to) the various tasks involved in your research and to set target dates for completion of each. You can then present this information in the form of a schedule that you can attach to your research proposal.

▶ Length

If a research proposal is required merely to demonstrate that students have devised an appropriate and workable research project, while consistent with this aim, the research proposal should be as short as possible. Only material that is necessary should be included, and the proposal should be written concisely. If no limit has been set, a maximum of about 2000 words should be taken as a guide. It should be possible to summarize any proposed research in a document of about this length.

On the other hand, sometimes students are required to demonstrate in their research proposals their knowledge of the area of research in some detail. In this case, the literature review that forms the introduction of the research proposal will be quite lengthy – probably in the order of about 6000 words.

▶ Content

A research proposal can be thought of a research report[2] written in advance and based upon an expected outcome. The only major difference between writing a research proposal and writing a research report, then, is that while the former is based upon what is known, the latter is based partly upon what is known and partly upon conjecture. In a research proposal, the research problem, question, and design are known, but the expected outcome is a matter of some conjecture.

▶ Structure

The structure of a research proposal is similar to that of a research report, but the headings used differ slightly.

Quantitative research

In the case of quantitative research, the parts involved in a research report are usually Introduction, Method, Results, and Discussion sections. However, in a research proposal you are presenting your intended research and data analysis, not reporting what you did; and your expected outcome, not what you found. Therefore, more appropriate headings should be used. The format of a research proposal for quantitative research involving a single experiment or study could, then, be of the form shown in Box 1.

Box 1   A possible format of a quantitative research proposal

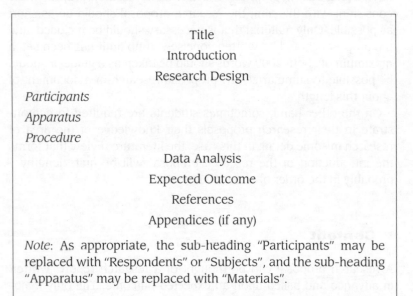

Title

Introduction

Research Design

Participants

Apparatus

Procedure

Data Analysis

Expected Outcome

References

Appendices (if any)

Note: As appropriate, the sub-heading "Participants" may be replaced with "Respondents" or "Subjects", and the sub-heading "Apparatus" may be replaced with "Materials".

Qualitative research

In principle, the format of a qualitative research proposal is the same as that for a quantitative research proposal. However, it will vary somewhat with the nature of the research involved, and some judgement is required. For example, it is often preferable to replace the sub-heading "Participants" with one that is more appropriate (e.g., "Sample"). In addition, apparatus will not be used in qualitative research, and so the heading "Apparatus" should be replaced with "Materials" if any were to be used, or perhaps simply deleted.

With only minor changes in the headings shown in Box 1, then, the format for a qualitative research proposal may be the same as that for quantitative research.

On the other hand, in some circumstances such simple modifications might not be adequate. As an example, it might be appropriate to use a heading such as "Setting" under which the setting of the research is described, and a heading such as "Characteristics of the Group" under which those involved in the research are described. In addition, it might be preferable to use a heading such as "Research Design and Method", and "Expected Findings" in lieu of "Expected Outcome". An alternative structure that could be appropriate for a qualitative research proposal, therefore, is as shown in Box 2.

Box 2   A possible format of a qualitative research proposal

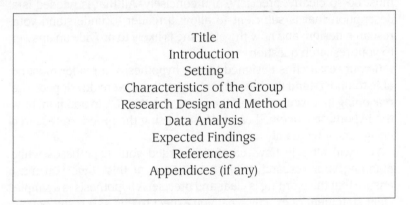

Title
Introduction
Setting
Characteristics of the Group
Research Design and Method
Data Analysis
Expected Findings
References
Appendices (if any)

▶ Planning and writing a research proposal

What is involved in the planning and writing of a research proposal and of a research report are very similar. However, there are some differences of which you need to be aware. The following notes, therefore, are provided to assist you with the planning and writing of your research proposal.

Introduction

You will already have read the relevant literature analytically and critically, and examined the relevant theory, research findings, and ideas. As a result, you will have developed your own ideas. In particular, you will have identified and defined a research problem, defined a research question, and designed the research that you intend to use to investigate that question. Therefore, you will have all of the information and ideas that you need to write the literature review that forms the introduction to your research proposal.

You must demonstrate that there is a valid research problem of some importance, and you must present it clearly, concisely, and convincingly. Having done this, you must present the research question that you intend to investigate and make clear how an answer to this question will potentially provide a solution or partial solution to the research problem being addressed. Where a theoretical hypothesis is involved, you must develop this on the basis of logical reasoning.

When describing in outline your intended research design, you must do so clearly, precisely, and concisely. All that is needed is a description that is sufficient to allow a reader to understand your research design, and how the outcome is likely to provide an answer to your research question.

If your research is designed to test hypotheses, a reader must be able to understand the basis upon which these were developed. The reasoning involved will be of the form, "If A then B". In addition, how the hypotheses involved can be tested using the proposed research design must be readily apparent.

You will already have carefully worded your hypotheses while planning your research project. However, at this stage you must ensure that the wording is clear and precise. A hypothesis is a simple, clear statement of exactly what you expect to find as a result of your manipulation of the independent variable(s) and measurement of the dependent variable(s).

If your intended research is of a qualitative nature, it may not be designed to test an explicit hypothesis. On the other hand, it is likely that you have some expectation in regard to the outcome. Where possible, you should present this expected outcome as you would a hypothesis in quantitative research. In any event, you must make clear the direction of your research and how you expect it to provide an answer to the research question that you are investigating, and so a solution or partial solution to the research problem that you are addressing.

Writing

When describing in outline the research design, this should be done using the present tense. You are arguing that this is a research design that can be used to investigate the research question. On the other hand, hypotheses are predictions of what you expect, and so are written in the future tense.

Research design

Because you will have designed your intended research in detail – including the necessary data analysis – you will have all of the information and ideas that you need to write what in a quantitative research report constitutes the Method and Results sections of your research proposal. The only difference is that the research design is being proposed, not reported as something that has been done. Where appropriate, you should give the expected or desired strength of effect, and discuss the power of your research design.

Put briefly, you must provide sufficient information so that the potential effectiveness of your research design can be assessed. This will include consideration of the operational definitions of variables that you have chosen, how you intend to measure them, and the validity of the measure that you intend to use. In the case of experimental research, it will also include consideration of the likely effectiveness of your intended manipulation of the independent variable(s).

The critical considerations in the case of quantitative research are: can the research hypothesis or hypotheses be effectively tested using this research design, and how will supporting the hypothesis or hypotheses to be tested provide an answer to the specific research question being investigated? Some proposed research fails in this regard. For example, one student wanted to address the problem of poor performance of motor skills, and he wanted to argue that this was caused by a perceptual dysfunction. However, his research design could only provide evidence of a relationship between the variables, and not necessarily evidence of causality.

If the intended research is of a qualitative nature, it may be that no explicit hypotheses are involved. In this case, the critical consideration is how the outcome of the research could potentially provide an answer to the research question being investigated. Sometimes proposed research of a qualitative nature fails in this regard because the research question has not been clearly defined. An example of this is provided by a research design that a student intended to use to investigate the content of reports on young offenders, which are written by psychologists for use in court. Although it was not clearly presented in her research proposal, this student's intention seemed to be to investigate the usefulness of psychologists' reports in court. However, she intended merely to test the content of a sample of reports against a list of criteria that she had prepared based on the content that several psychologists had previously suggested should be included. Her findings, therefore, could only reveal any difference between what she had predicted should be included in such reports and what was included. Clearly, this outcome could not present an answer to her apparent research question.

Writing

While the Method section of a research report is written in the past tense, because you are expressing your present intention, the Research Design section of a research proposal should usually be written in the present tense. In some circumstance, however, the future tense can be appropriate. It is also acceptable to use first person personal pronouns. Therefore, you could write, for example, something like, "I intend to test participants in three conditions", or "I will select the participants from. ..."

Data analysis

This section is similar to the Results section in a quantitative research report. The difference is that you are describing your intended data analysis. You must do this in sufficient detail to allow a reader to assess its appropriateness. In the case of experimental research, the critical question that a reader will ask is: can the research hypothesis or hypotheses be effectively and validly tested using the proposed analysis?

Explicit hypotheses may not be involved in qualitative research, and so the question of testing them will not apply. In addition, because of the flexible nature of this form of research, the necessity for some analyses might not be evident when it is planned and so cannot be proposed at this point. Nonetheless, at least an intended form of initial data analysis must be given, and the critical question will be: how can the intended analysis be used to provide an answer to the research question being investigated?

The reason for any intended analysis must be readily apparent, and it must serve some useful purpose. Students sometimes overlook the necessity of relating their proposed data analyses to their research questions, and those that they propose seem to be in the form of a "fishing expedition". For instance, one student, who had predicted a simple difference between scores on two sets of variables in two conditions, proposed analysing his data using four t tests, analysis of variance, and correlation analyses. In this case, an analysis of variance would have been sufficient.

Writing

It is usual to write the Data Analysis section in the present tense because you are expressing what you presently intend to do; or, if appropriate, in the future tense. It is also acceptable to use first person personal pronouns. Therefore, in this section you could write something like, "I intend to analyse the data using a 2×2 (Stress $\times$ Accuracy) repeated design analysis of variance."

When proposing any data analysis, you must also indicate its purpose. For example, you could write something like, "To test the hypothesis that fatigue will result in lengthened reaction time, I intend to use a t test." Giving the purpose for analyses shows that you know what you intend to test for, and that you are not simply hoping that something will "show up" in the course of your proposed analyses.

Expected outcome

This section is closely associated with the Data Analysis section. Here, you are presenting an outline of the expected outcome of your research. Of course, because this involves some conjecture, you cannot present specific details such as statistics. Rather, you can only predict an expected pattern of results.

If the intended research involves the testing of hypotheses, you will expect these to be supported and so you will have some expected pattern of results in mind. For example, this might be a difference or relationship, a particular interaction, or some other pattern of results. In the case of qualitative research, it may be that no explicit hypothesis is involved. On the other hand, you will probably have some expectations in regard to the outcome. For instance, you might have followed some reasoning process in a form such as, "If people ... then they should ...". As an example, if you were investigating the reaction of people to some natural disaster, you could expect that they would experience some difficulty in coping with the resultant trauma.

Whatever the form of the anticipated outcome, you should demonstrate how you expect this to provide an answer to the research question being investigated, and so a potential solution to the research problem being addressed. Therefore, you will have to relate your expected outcome to the theory, ideas, and previous research in the area that are referred to in your introduction. In the case of qualitative research, where appropriate, you should suggest how the outcome of your research might contribute to the development of a theory.

You should also show how your research is expected to fulfil the scientific goals of description and explanation, preferably prediction, and ideally control. In addition, you should suggest how you expect the outcome of your research to add to knowledge in the area. For instance, you might expect that it will extend the findings of earlier work in some particular way, suggest a solution to some practical problem, or perhaps question the validity of some theory.

Writing

When writing this section, it is appropriate to use first person personal pronouns and the present tense. For example, you could write something like, "I expect to find a significant difference between choice and simple reaction times." However, the past tense may also be used. For instance, you might write something like, "Oliver and Twist (2002) found.... Consistent with this, I expect....".

▶ **Figures and tables**

When preparing a research proposal, you should always consider the possible use of figures and/or tables. For example, some information, such as details of intended participants can be summarized in the form of a table, or a figure could provide a useful supplement to a description of some apparatus or experimental task that you intend to use. In particular, it is often advisable, if not necessary, to use illustrations such as graphs, diagrams, or maps to allow a reader to understand your expected outcome. This is particularly so when you are predicting a pattern of results such as an interaction or some other complex interrelationship between variables.

▶ Drafts of research proposals

As for anything that anyone writes, a number of drafts of a research proposal will be needed. You will, in particular, need to edit these for content. In addition, you will need to edit your research proposal for grammar, spelling, punctuation, and editorial style. Like any other paper, a research proposal must be written in a scholarly manner, and must comply with the necessary editorial style requirements.

You may, and probably will, submit one or two drafts of your research proposal to your supervisor. However, you should not expect your supervisor to read numerous drafts – two is usually an acceptable maximum. In any event, the time available will preclude you from submitting a number of drafts.

▶ Pilot or validation research

It is always a good idea to carry out pilot research in the form of a "test run" with a view to detecting any unforeseen problems with the research design. There is no need to refer to such intended pilot research in a research proposal. On the other hand, when pilot research is carried out for some specific purpose, such as testing the effectiveness of the manipulation of an independent variable, the planned pilot research must be included in the research proposal as an entity in its own right. By its nature, validation research is carried out for a specific purpose, and so it will always be reported separately.

When a research project involves pilot research for a specific purpose or validation research, the structure of the research proposal will not differ greatly from that for one that does not. Essentially, the only difference is the addition of the pilot or validation research.

Structure

All that is needed when planning the structure of a research proposal that involves pilot or validation research is to add the pilot or validation research before the experiment or study proper.[3] An example of the format for such a research proposal is given in Box 3.

Box 3 Possible format of a research proposal involving pilot or validation research

Title

Introduction

Pilot (Validation) Research

Introduction

Research Design

Participants

Apparatus

Procedure

Data Analysis

Expected Outcome

Experiment (Study)

Introduction

Research Design

Participants

Apparatus

Procedure

Data Analysis

Expected Outcome

Overall Expected Outcome

References

Appendices (if any)

Note: Often, it is appropriate to combine the Data Analysis and Expected Outcome sections of the pilot or validation research into one section.

Planning

What is involved in the planning of a research proposal that includes pilot or validation research does not differ markedly from that involved in one that does not. However, the pilot or validation research must be considered as a separate experiment or study.

Introduction to a research proposal

The introduction to a research proposal that involves pilot or validation research essentially does not differ from that for one that does not. The only requirement is the addition of a brief explanation of why the pilot or validation research is believed to be necessary, and what it is intended to achieve.

Introduction to the pilot or validation research

Although part of the research project, pilot or validation research is a separate experiment or study. It must, therefore, have its own short introduction that can be understood in its own right. Because, however, relevant material will have been discussed in detail in the introduction to the research proposal, it need only be briefly referred to in the introduction to the pilot or validation research. On the other hand, the expected outcome of this research must be given clearly. If hypotheses are to be tested, these must be developed and presented as they would normally be.

Introduction to the research proper

The introduction to the research proper will include only brief reference to material included in the introduction to the research proposal, and so it will be short. It must, however, include appropriate reference to the expected outcome of the pilot or validation research. For example, in the case of pilot research such a reference might be to the expected effectiveness of the manipulation of some independent variable, or in the case of validation research to the expected validity of some instrument. Of course, such references can, at this point, only be made on the basis of conjecture. They might, therefore, be phrased in the form of, "Presuming that....".

Overall expected outcome

Planning of the Overall Expected Outcome section of a research proposal that includes pilot or validation research involves similar planning to that for the Expected Outcome section of one that does not. Again, this can be done only on the basis of conjecture. In particular, it can only be based on the assumption that the pilot or validation research was successful, and that the outcome of the experiment or study proper was as expected.

▶ Multiple experiments or studies

In principle, a research proposal for a project that involves multiple experiments or studies does not differ markedly from one that involves only a single experiment or study. Essentially, the only difference is that the description of the proposed research is somewhat more complex and based upon more conjecture.

Structure

The structure of a research proposal for a project that includes several experiments or studies is relatively straightforward. An example of a possible format for a research project involving two experiments is given in Box 4.[4]

Box 4 Possible format of a research proposal involving multiple experiments or studies

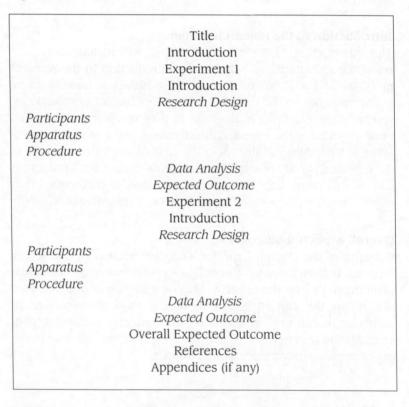

Title

Introduction

Experiment 1

Introduction

Research Design

Participants

Apparatus

Procedure

Data Analysis

Expected Outcome

Experiment 2

Introduction

Research Design

Participants

Apparatus

Procedure

Data Analysis

Expected Outcome

Overall Expected Outcome

References

Appendices (if any)

Planning

Planning a research proposal that involves multiple experiments or studies involves the same considerations that are involved in the planning of one that involves only a single experiment or study. On the other hand, the outcome of the first experiment or study can only be predicted on the basis of conjecture. It is typically impossible, therefore, to propose in detail the experiments or studies that are planned to follow the first, and often the number of experiments or studies to be carried out cannot be predicted with certainty. When preparing a proposal for a research project involving multiple experiments or studies, therefore, it is probable that only the first can be proposed in detail, and the second in general terms – presuming that the outcome of the first will be as expected. Because of the accumulated conjecture involved, it is most likely that any further intended experiments or studies can only be proposed in very general terms.

Introduction to a research proposal

The introduction to a research proposal that involves multiple experiments or studies essentially does not differ from that for one that does not. The only difference is that neither the outline designs of the research nor research hypotheses to be tested can be included. The introduction to the research proposal can only refer in general terms to the intended experiments or studies.

Introduction to individual experiments or studies

Each proposed individual experiment or study will have its own short introduction. This will include only brief reference to the relevant material that has been discussed in detail in the introduction to the research proposal. It will, however, include an adequately detailed outline research design for the experiment or study and, where appropriate, the hypotheses to be tested will be developed and presented in the normal manner.

▶ A word of advice

Writing a research proposal should not be unduly difficult if you have carefully designed and planned your research. On the other hand, it will be time consuming and because you will, no doubt, be keen to begin your data collection, the requirement to do so can be a little frustrating. There are, however, benefits associated with the writing of a research proposal.

Because writing and thinking are intimately related, the requirement to write a research proposal will force you to consider your proposed research carefully and in detail. Doing this should allow you to detect any flaws in your reasoning and any potential problem that might arise. In particular, writing a research proposal forces you to define clearly the research problem that you are addressing and the research question that you are investigating. Where appropriate, it also forces you to write clearly and concisely any hypotheses involved, and to develop clearly the logical reasoning that leads to them. Finally, writing a research proposal forces you to consider the expected outcome of your research, and how this could provide an answer to the research question that you are investigating, and so a potential solution to the research problem that you are addressing.

8 A Research Proposal Seminar

In some programmes of study, students are required to present their research proposals in the form of a seminar. The purpose of this requirement is to ensure that students are fully prepared before they begin to collect data for their research. In addition, presenting an oral research proposal allows students the opportunity to benefit from comments and suggestions made by those present, and so perhaps improve their proposed research or avoid some potential problem. While students will have carefully planned their proposed research and discussed it with their supervisors, it is always possible that something has been overlooked. More commonly, however, because the audience will view the proposed research from a fresh perspective, new and useful ideas might be suggested.

▶ Anxiety

Some students, particularly those who are enrolled in a masters or professional doctorate programme, might previously have presented a number of seminars. The majority of students, however, will have presented only a few, and perhaps only to an audience comprising fellow students and a single academic who was teaching the course, subject, module, or unit in which this was a requirement. To most students, therefore, the prospect of presenting a seminar to a group that includes several academics will result in some anxiety.

Everyone approaches addressing a group with some trepidation. This is only natural. However, there should be no need for undue anxiety. You will already have prepared and planned your research in detail, and you will have discussed it with your supervisor. Consequently, you should be confident that you have developed an appropriate and viable piece of research, and you will be intimately familiar with it. All that you need to do, then, is to present your proposed research to the audience.

Most likely, your audience will comprise a small number of academics from the department and at least some of your fellow students. The academics will be present partly out of interest, but mainly with a view to offering possibly helpful comments and suggestions. Your fellow students will no doubt be present because they are encouraged or required to be so, but they too will be interested in your proposed research – and, because they too will have to present their own research proposals, they will be sympathetic. Of course, your supervisor will already be familiar with your intended research, but he or she will be present to provide you with some "moral" and, if need be, practical support. The point is that no one will be present with the intention of being critical. Rather, they will try to be helpful. Understanding this should help you to overcome, or at least minimize, your natural trepidation.

▶ Content

The content of your research proposal should not present you with any difficulty. You will already have designed and planned your intended research in detail, and you will most likely have prepared a written research proposal. Even if a written research proposal was not required, you would have been wise to have prepared one.

If you wrote a research proposal that included a lengthy literature review, you will not be able to present all of the material included in it at your seminar. Rather, you will only be able to present important material that is critical to an understanding of your proposed research. If you have written a lengthy research proposal, you would be wise to edit and rewrite it to a length not exceeding about 2000 words. Whilst you should not read your research proposal, writing it in within this limit will force you to restrict the content to that which could be orally presented in about 20 minutes.

You might think that it is impossible to describe your proposed research adequately within such a short word length limit. If so, you should consider that authors of journal articles typically are required to write a summary (usually described as an abstract) of their reported research within a limit of no more than about 150 words – and, no doubt, you will have had some experience with writing an abstract. In addition, you should consider that eventually you will have to write an abstract (or summary) of your research for your thesis – within a limit of perhaps no more than 250–300 words. To give you some guide to how to summarize a piece of research, therefore, you might like to read some abstracts of journal articles and of theses submitted by previous students.

On the other hand, your research proposal will include more detail than is included in an abstract. In particular, you will need to begin by presenting a concise review of the relevant literature (including only important theory, ideas, and previous research findings); and from this, show how you identified the research problem that you are addressing. Then, if you are describing a proposed piece of experimental research, you need to

1. Define the research problem that you are addressing.
2. Define the research question that you intend to investigate.
3. Where appropriate, give your theoretical hypothesis and explain how this was developed.
4. Describe in outline your intended research design.
5. Where appropriate, give the research hypotheses you intend to test, and explain how these were developed.
6. Describe the data analyses that you intend to use, and give their purpose.
7. Outline the expected outcome.
8. Explain how you think the expected outcome will provide an answer to the research question, and so a solution or partial solution to the research problem addressed.

If your proposed research is of a qualitative nature, there may be no explicit theoretical or research hypotheses. When this is so, if possible, you should give some indication of the expected outcome. In any event, you must demonstrate how you expect the outcome to provide a solution or partial solution to the research problem addressed.

▶ Preparation

Because you will be intimately familiar with the needed content of your research proposal seminar, you should be able to approach your presentation with confidence. Nonetheless, you will have to carry out the necessary preparation.

Notes

You should not simply read your research proposal to the audience. If you were to adopt this approach, you would do better to distribute written copies of your proposal to the audience and then await questions. There is nothing likely to be more boring for an audience than listening to a number of students consecutively reading their research proposals. Remember, you are presenting your seminar with the prospect of gaining helpful feedback. Therefore, the last thing you want to do is to bore your audience. In any event, you need to demonstrate that you know what you intend to do, not that you can read. There is, then, no point in writing your seminar in the form of a script. On the other hand, you will, no doubt, want to prepare some notes on key points.

Notes can be used as a memory aid and to ensure that you do not "go off track", or forget some point. You might, for example, make notes of some important research findings or ideas. In addition, you might like to write in detail your definitions of the research problem and question, operational definitions of variables, or of hypotheses to be tested, so that you can read these if you think it advisable or necessary.

Visual aids

Sometimes, you might want to present written material in the form of a visual aid. For instance, you might like to present a list of key points, your research problem, some definition, or your research hypotheses in this form. Written material presented in this manner must be very brief – no more than perhaps about 25 words. Usually, however, visual aids are in the form of illustrations, such as a diagram of the layout of apparatus or perhaps a map. Most commonly, they will be in the form of graphs or diagrams used to illustrate expected outcomes in the form of some relationship(s) between variables.

If you wrote a research proposal, you should already have prepared any necessary illustrations. For the purposes of a seminar, however, visual aids need to be prepared in a form that allows them to be shown to a group. Usually, this means preparing an overhead slide (acetate) or using an appropriate computer programme and projector.

A blackboard or whiteboard can be used as a visual aid, but this should be avoided. Writing or drawing takes time, which is at a premium. In addition, the product is often untidy and possibly illegible. On the other hand, a blackboard or whiteboard can be useful for impromptu illustrations when answering questions.

Time

The time allowed for a seminar can vary, but typically you will be allowed 20 minutes to present your research proposal, followed by 10 minutes for question and discussion. This time allocation must not be exceeded. Other students will have been scheduled to present their research proposals on the same day, and only a limited time will have been allotted to this. Consequently, if you exceed your allowed time, one or more other students will have less available.

Do not, as did one student, begin your presentation by announcing that you will exceed the allowed time and apologizing for doing so. This showed the student's complete disregard for the requirements given to him in relation to time. More importantly, it showed his disregard for his fellow students who then had less time available for their presentations. His announcement was not well received by the audience and, no doubt, did not encourage them to try to be helpful.

You might be permitted to exceed your presentation time by 1 or 2 minutes, but exceeding that allowed limit will reduce the time available for questions and discussion. As has already been pointed out, the main purpose of presenting a research proposal seminar is to allow you to benefit from questions, comments, or suggestions from the audience.

Rehearsal

You must rehearse your presentation. This is necessary if you are to present your research proposal confidently, without "stumbles", and within the allowed time.

It is advisable that you first rehearse in an empty room, or perhaps with a ruminating cow as an audience. While you might feel somewhat foolish when doing this, it does avoid the potential embarrassment that would otherwise result when you inevitably stumble. Perhaps, you have seen one of those "blooper" shows on television. Unlike a television production, however, you will be presenting live, and so will not be able to do a "re-take".

The first rehearsal is intended only to ensure that you can present the necessary material in the time allowed. Typically, you will exceed this, and so you will have to summarize or delete some material. No doubt, you will find that you have to repeat this process several times.

When you are confident that you can "fit within" the allowed time, you should try to rehearse your presentation in front of an audience. Your fellow students, who are faced with the same task, will no doubt co-operate – and you can return the favour. If possible, your final rehearsal should be in the room in which you have to present your proposal. This will help you to feel more comfortable and aid your memory on "the day".

▶ Confidence

You should approach your presentation as simply describing your intended research to a group of colleagues with a view to having them comment on it. In particular, you want to become aware of any potential problems or any possible improvements before you begin to collect data. Once again, remember that the academics in the audience are there to help you. It is, of course, also possible that one of your fellow students might make a helpful suggestion.

Although you will no doubt experience some anxiety, as has already been pointed out, you will know what you want to communicate to the audience. In addition, you will have prepared your presentation and rehearsed it. You should, therefore, be able to approach your presentation with confidence. On the other hand, it is wise not to be overconfident, or to create the impression of being so. One British yachtsman invented a motto for the coasters that he used on his yacht, which reads, "nobo dylo vesas martarse".

▶ Presentation

Although you will no doubt have had some experience with presenting a seminar, some tips might be useful.

Treat your audience with respect. They will have taken the time to attend your seminar, and they will want to help you. You can show respect by a neat and tidy personal appearance, and by making eye contact with individual members of the audience from time to time.

Speak confidently, clearly, and a little more slowly than normal. Vary your tone and rhythm when speaking: nothing is more boring than a dull monotone. You can also use tone of voice to emphasize a point, and it is a good idea to pause briefly at important points to allow the audience to consider them.

If you want to read something from your notes, do so. Do not try to hide the fact that you are reading. Hiding notes in the palm of the hand and trying to read them surreptitiously is ridiculous and fools no one. Similarly, when you simply refer to your notes, do not try to hide the fact. There is nothing wrong with referring to notes. In any event, it is far better to do so than to become confused and "lose track" with the possible result of omitting some important point.

When using visual aids do not rush. Point out salient features such as headings on a table, places on a map, or key points in a photograph. In the case of graphs, point out the labels on axes and the curves, and explain any key aspects such as an interaction. Pause briefly to allow the audience to consider what is illustrated, and then carry on with any necessary explanation and discussion. When you have ended your comments, remove the visual aid: if you do not, you will find some members of the audience will continue to look at it for a time, and not listen to you.

How you end your presentation is a matter of individual preference. One option is to say something like, "This concludes my presentation. Thank you for your attention." However, if your presentation ends with a short statement that clearly indicates that it has ended, there is obviously no need to say that it has. In this case, it is adequate to say, "Thank you for your attention", or perhaps simply, "Thank you". Of course, if you have not rehearsed well and you misjudge the time, you will have no option. Rather, whoever is chairing the seminar will ask you to stop. This can be embarrassing, not to mention resulting in an incomplete presentation.

▶ A final note

The academics present at your seminar will understand your nervousness. Once, they were in the same position as you are now: and, no doubt, they will have made the occasional slip when presenting papers at seminars and conferences. Your fellow students, of course, will be sympathetic. No one present, therefore, will expect you to present a perfect seminar. On the other hand, your audience will expect a reasonable effort. This can be achieved if you believe that you have devised a good piece of research, know what you want to convey to the audience, and have prepared and rehearsed well.

Typically, the best actors and performers report that they approach any performance with at least some "stage fright", and some suggest that this improves their performance. There is, then, no reason why you should be surprised if you are nervous when confronted with the task of presenting a research proposal seminar. Try to believe in yourself, and try not to be afraid of the audience. The beginning is the hard part. It is a little like getting pickled onions out a jar: The first one is hard to get – the rest come easily.

9 The Structure and Format of a Thesis

Before you begin to write your thesis, you need to plan its structure. This will give direction to your writing: you will know what parts are needed and their function. In addition, knowing the structure of your thesis will allow you to plan time for writing its parts.

You will also have to consider the format of your thesis because structure and format are interrelated: one can influence the other. The format that you use might be specified as a requirement or left to your discretion.

▶ The basic structure

The number of parts and sub-parts in a thesis will vary, but there will always be three main parts: the introduction, a report of the research carried out, and a discussion. The only difference in the basic structure of theses, therefore, is in the structure of the part in which the research that has been carried out is reported. This will differ somewhat between quantitative and qualitative research. It will also differ depending on whether or not pilot or validation research is involved, and on the number of experiments or studies reported.

Single experiment or study

If the research involves only a single experiment or study of a quantitative nature, the basic structure of your thesis will not differ from that of the research reports[1] that you will have written in the past. In this case, the basic structure required will be that which is shown in Box 1.

Box 1 Basic structure of a quantitative thesis involving only a single experiment or study

Abstract
Introduction
Method

Participants
Apparatus
Procedure

Results
Discussion
Appendices

Note: As appropriate, the sub-heading "Participants" may be replaced with "Respondents" or "Subjects", and the sub-heading "Apparatus" may be replaced with "Materials".

The structure of a thesis involving only a single study of a qualitative nature will be similar to that of one involving a single experiment or study of a quantitative nature. It is likely, however, that the headings used will differ slightly. For instance, it might be more appropriate to use "Sample" instead of "Participants", and because no apparatus will be used, the heading "Materials" might be appropriate.

In some instances, it might be more appropriate to adopt a slightly different structure with suitable headings. For example, rather than "Method", it might be more appropriate to use "Research Design and Method", or perhaps simply "Research Design", as a heading. An alternative possible structure of a qualitative thesis is given in Box 2.

Because of the variable nature of qualitative research, the formats suggested above might well not be suitable for a particular thesis. For example, the findings might be partly interpreted in the Findings section, and more fully discussed in the Discussion section. In this case, the heading "Findings and Preliminary Analysis", for instance, could be used. Alternatively, it might be more appropriate to combine the Findings and Discussion sections. You would be well advised to discuss possible formats with your supervisor.

Box 2   An possible format of a qualitative thesis involving a single study

Abstract
Introduction
Setting
Characteristics of the Group
Research Design and Method
Findings
Discussion
References
Appendices

Pilot or validation research

If you were to carry out pilot research for a specific purpose, or validation research, the basic structure of your thesis will differ only slightly from those suggested for a thesis involving only a single experiment or study. All that is required is the addition of the pilot or validation research before the research proper. Such preliminary research will be in the form of an experiment or study, and so the same headings and sub-headings that would be used for any experiment or study are needed. To distinguish any preliminary research from the research proper, however, the heading "Pilot Research" or "Validation Research" is commonly used.

An example of the possible structure of a thesis that includes pilot or validation research is given in Box 3. This example is based on research of a quantitative nature, but the principles involved apply equally to a thesis based on research of a qualitative nature.

Multiple experiments or studies

The structure of a thesis that includes multiple experiments or studies is often expected to be much more complex than that of a thesis that does not. This expected complexity, however, is more apparent than real. Essentially, all that is involved is a

Box 3   Example basic structure of a thesis involving pilot research

Abstract
Introduction

Pilot (Validation) Research
Introduction

Participants
Apparatus
Procedure

Results
Discussion

Experiment
Introduction
Method

Participants
Apparatus
Procedure

Results
Discussion

Discussion
Appendices

Notes:

1. For the pilot or validation research, it is often convenient to combine the Results and Discussion sections under the heading "Results and Discussion".

2. As appropriate, the sub-heading "Participants" may be replaced with "Respondents" or "Subjects", and the sub-heading "Apparatus" may be replaced with "Materials".

series of experiments or studies with appropriate headings and sub-headings. The only real difference is that each experiment or study begins with its own relatively brief introduction and ends with a discussion, or perhaps a combined results and discussion section. In addition, the discussion section of the thesis is usually described as a "General Discussion" in which the overall outcome of the series of experiments or studies involved is discussed. An example of the basic structure of such a thesis is given in Box 4.

Box 4 Example basic structure of a thesis involving multiple experiments

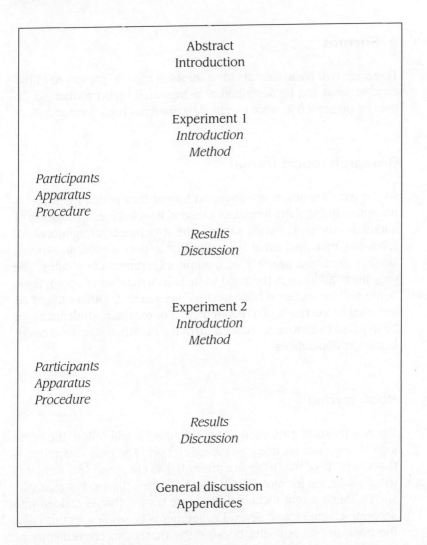

Abstract
Introduction

Experiment 1
Introduction
Method

Participants
Apparatus
Procedure

Results
Discussion

Experiment 2
Introduction
Method

Participants
Apparatus
Procedure

Results
Discussion

General discussion
Appendices

BOX 4 (Continued)

Notes:
1. As appropriate, the sub-heading "Participants" may be replaced with "Respondents" or "Subjects", and the sub-heading "Apparatus" may be replaced with "Materials".
2. In some circumstances, the results and discussion for individual experiments or studies can be combined under the heading "Results and Discussion".

▶ Format

There are two basic formats for a thesis: it may be presented in the form of what can be described as a "research report format"; or, it may be presented in what can be described as "book format".

Research report format

As the term implies, research report format means that the thesis is presented in the same format as a research report (i.e., in the form of a journal article). For such a thesis, the structure is straightforward, following that applicable to a research report involving either a single experiment or study, or multiple experiments or studies. The only likely addition is the need to include a number of appendices. Some will be included because they are needed. Others might be included as the result of a requirement. For example, students might be required to include raw data and/or the output of statistical calculations as appendices.

Book format

When a thesis is presented in book format, it will follow the same logical sequence as does a research report. The only difference is that the parts of the thesis are presented as chapters. This format is usually adopted for more lengthy and complex theses. For example, such a thesis might include a literature review that is divided into separate chapters, and several experiments or studies. In this case, the book format is useful because the thesis can conveniently be organized into chapters relating to its various parts. For instance, Chapter 1 could be a literature review, Chapter 2 a critical review of methods used in earlier research, Chapter 3 Experiment 1, Chapter 4 Experiment 2, and so on. Again, it is likely that appendices will be needed, and students might be required to include specified material as appendices.

Deciding on a format

If you are free to choose between formats, you should make your decision on the basis of the length and complexity of your thesis. In some instances, it may be that, although only a single experiment or study is involved, the thesis is lengthy and/or complex, and so lends itself to division into parts in the form of chapters.

▶ Chapters of a thesis in book format

Most commonly, book format is used when the introduction is lengthy and the reported research involves more than a single experiment or study. In such a thesis, the introduction could be divided into chapters with titles such as "Introduction", "Previous Research Approaches", and "Research Design". Using these chapter titles, and for a thesis involving pilot research and multiple experiments, the format of a thesis could be as shown in Box 5.

Box 5 Example basic structure of a complex thesis in book format

Chapter	Title
	Abstract
1	Introduction
2	Previous Research Approaches
3	Research Design
4	Pilot Research
5	Experiment 1
6	Experiment 2
7	Experiment 3
8	General Discussion
	References
	Appendices

The number of chapters in a thesis will vary with its needs. As a guide, however, it is normally advisable to divide a lengthy introduction into two or more chapters. In addition, if the reported research involves multiple experiments or studies, it is usual to report each in a separate chapter, in which case the general discussion will be presented as a separate chapter.

▶ Structure of the parts

Although the basic structure of theses is essentially common, there will be variations in the structure of the individual parts. Having planned its basic structure, you then have to plan the structure of each of the individual parts of your thesis. Commonly, this is done immediately before beginning to write the part involved. In any event, you will first plan the introduction, then the research part of your thesis, and finally the discussion. If your research involves a pilot or validation experiment or study, and/or multiple experiments or studies, you will have to plan these sub-parts of your thesis progressively as you advance with your work.

10 Writing a Thesis

When the research component of a programme of study must be completed in a single year, it is usually examined solely on the basis of the thesis that is submitted. The most common departure from this arises when, in addition to the thesis, students are required to submit a substantial literature review or a written research proposal that includes a substantial literature review. In such circumstances, the assessment of the research component is divided between the two items. This latter approach is often adopted in two-year programmes in which the research component is divided into two parts that are variously referred to as courses, subjects, modules, or units. In any event, the thesis always contributes at least very substantially to the assessment of the research component of the programme of study. It must, therefore, be well written. Sometimes, students do not fully appreciate this, and they do not devote sufficient time and effort to the writing of their theses.

It also needs to be understood that, although it might be divided into two parts, the research component remains as an entity. In particular, when a separate literature review is submitted either as a free-standing item or as part of a research proposal, it forms an integral part of the research. When this happens, the introduction to the thesis will effectively comprise a revision of the earlier submitted literature review or an abbreviated version of it. The latter typically occurs when the thesis is required to be in the form of a journal article.

The advice offered here is based on the assumption that the research component of a programme of study is to be examined solely on the basis of the thesis that is submitted. However, if you understand that the research component is an entity, you will appreciate that the advice offered is equally applicable when this component is divided into two parts.

▶ Requirements of a thesis

Put simply, in the research component of any programme of study, students are expected to investigate effectively a research problem that is of some importance and to propose some solution or partial solution to it. The basic requirements of a thesis, then, are that it demonstrates that the student has

- identified and defined a research problem that is of some importance,
- defined an appropriate research question,
- devised and carried out suitable research to investigate this question,
- used appropriate techniques to analyse the data collected,
- interpreted correctly the outcome of the analyses used, and
- proposed a valid solution or partial solution to the research problem.[1]

In addition to achieving these objectives, the thesis should also demonstrate that the research carried out has achieved the scientific goals of description and explanation, preferably prediction, and ideally the possibility of control. It should also demonstrate that the research has added to human knowledge, which requires that it must involve some originality.

Apart from fulfilling the requirements given above, a thesis must also demonstrate the student's ability to evaluate analytically and critically relevant research, ideas, and theory. It must show how the student's research follows from and builds upon existing theory and previous research in the area. Finally, a thesis should demonstrate an understanding of the development, role, application, and limitations of relevant theory.

▶ Examination

How a thesis is examined varies with the programme of study and with the policies and procedures adopted by a department. Typically, however, a thesis is examined independently by two academics who were not directly involved in the student's research. In some programmes, both examiners are external to the university, while in others one or both may be staff members in the department in which the student is studying.

Ideally, both examiners should be familiar with the area of research, but this is not always practical. It is possible, therefore, that one examiner – who is very familiar with the area – will detect a flaw in a thesis that another will not. On the other hand, it is also possible that an examiner who lacks expertise in the area will not recognize some novel aspect of the research that as been reported. In any event, because examiners will be influenced by the quality of theses that they have previously marked, their individual expectations of students' abilities, and their understanding of the expected standard of students' performance at the relevant level of study, examining a thesis will always involve an aspect of subjectivity. It is, therefore, possible that the grades recommended by examiners will differ.

In many institutions, if the difference between recommended grades is small, they are averaged; but, if the difference is large, a third examiner is appointed to overcome the problem. In other institutions, examiners initially recommend a provisional mark, after which they meet to discuss the thesis and to agree upon a final mark. Such procedures are designed to ensure that students' theses are fairly examined, and that any unduly generous or harsh marking is avoided.

The point that you need to understand is that your thesis will typically be examined by two (and possibly three) academics who were not directly involved in your research and who most likely do not know you. Consequently, you cannot expect that any allowance will be made for difficulties that you encountered while carrying out your research, or that credit will be given for your personal qualities, such as enthusiasm or ability to overcome problems. More importantly, your thesis must effectively communicate the necessary information and ideas to readers who were not directly involved in your research and so are not familiar with it.

If you think that your thesis is likely to be examined by an academic who does not have expertise in the area of your research, you should consider its writing carefully. In particular, you should ensure that the introduction and discussion parts very clearly convey and support your ideas. To achieve this, you might include somewhat more detail that you otherwise would.

▶ Information and ideas

Often, the terms *information* and *idea* are taken to be synonyms, and so are used interchangeably. For the present purposes, however, it is helpful to distinguish between information and ideas.

Information can be thought of as what might be described as "factual" material. This could include, for example, the details of participants in an experiment, the procedure followed in a piece of research, or statistics. By comparison, an idea can be thought of as a mental representation that provides an explanation, or possible explanation, of some phenomenon. One form of idea is a construct, such as gravity or intelligence. More commonly, ideas are in the form of proposed relationships – often of a causal nature. These proposed relationships may be between items of information, other ideas, or both. For example, a hypothesis is an idea, as is a theory – which can be thought of as a "grand idea".

It is important to understand that information is useful only in so much as it leads to some idea. For instance, information such as details of the procedure followed in an experiment, or of the statistical techniques employed when analysing data, can lead to the idea that some piece of research is flawed. As another example, information in the form of a statistical correlation can suggest an idea in the form of a proposed relationship between variables.

▶ Ideas in a thesis

Apart from being used to refer to the document that you submit as part of the requirements of your programme of study, a thesis means a proposition, and so an idea. It is your proposed solution or partial solution to the research problem addressed. This must be developed using a process of logical reasoning based on sound evidence – as is any other idea.

You will have developed a number of ideas in the process of devising and carrying out your research. Initially, based on the information and ideas that you found in the literature, you will have developed the idea of a particular research problem, and from this you will have developed the idea of an appropriate research question to investigate. Then, you will have developed the idea of a research design that can be used to investigate this question, and an idea of how to analyse the data to be collected. In due course, based on the information that you gathered in the form of the data collected and your analysis of it, you will have developed an idea in the form of an interpretation of the outcome. Finally, you will have developed the idea of a solution or partial solution to the research problem. Others will also be involved, but these are the main ideas.

Your written thesis, then, comprises a series of interconnected ideas upon which you base the reasoning that leads to your central idea, which is your thesis. You should be able to present your thesis clearly and concisely in the form of a single sentence.

The point is that, while the thesis that you write is an account of your research, it is not merely an account of what you did and found – which is simply information. Rather, it constitutes a series of ideas that you have developed on the basis of information derived from previous research, existing ideas (some in the form of theory), and information in the form of the findings of your research. These ideas are developed and presented in the appropriate parts of the thesis.

It is important for you to appreciate fully that in your thesis you are attempting to communicate your ideas to the reader. If you do not do this well, you will not achieve your goal, which is to communicate your thesis. You need to understand that, no matter how innovative or important, an idea is of no value unless it is effectively communicated.

▶ Parts of the thesis

A thesis will always have three main parts: the introduction, a report of the research carried out, and a discussion. Some research will involve a pilot or validation experiment or study, and some will involve multiple experiments or studies each of which will have its own short introduction and discussion. Nonetheless, there will always be an introduction to the research as an entity, a description of the research carried out and the resultant findings, and a discussion of the outcome.

▶ Length of the parts

It is impossible to stipulate how long any part of a thesis should be: it has to be as long as is needed to achieve its purpose. Too often, students ask supervisors something like, "Is this the right length?" or "How long should this part be?" There can be no "correct" answer to such questions. As a rough guide, in a thesis reporting only a single experiment or study, the proportions allotted to the introduction, research, and discussion parts should perhaps be of the order of 50, 20, and 30% respectively. However, when a thesis involves pilot or validation research, or multiple experiments or studies, each will have its own short introduction (in addition to the introduction proper) and discussion (or perhaps a results and discussion section), and so the proportions suggested will change somewhat. In any event, there will be instances in which this rule of thumb is not applicable. For example, the introduction might be very straightforward, but the research very complex, and so less space is needed for the former and more for the latter. In general, however, the introduction and discussion parts of a thesis will form its bulk, with the former usually being somewhat longer than the latter.

If the reported research is of a qualitative nature, some discussion of findings may be included in the research part of the thesis, and so the discussion proper may be shorter than would be the case in a thesis based on quantitative research. On the other hand, it is sometimes more appropriate to combine the findings and discussion sections in a qualitative thesis. In this case, the "discussion" could be longer than it would otherwise be.

All that can be done when writing a thesis, then, is to estimate the proportion of the allowed word length that can be made available to a particular part. This will usually result in a satisfactory outcome. In some instances, however, it might ultimately prove to be necessary to rewrite one or more of its parts to make the thesis in its entirety fit within the allowed word limit.

▶ Planning

The information and ideas in a thesis must be presented in a logical sequence. To use the analogy of building a house – the foundation must be laid before the walls can be built on them, and these must be completed before the roof can be added. For example, in the introduction you might first discuss the research methods or paradigm used when developing some theory, then critically examine the theory. This might lead you to question the validity of some aspect of the theory. In turn, this leads you to the ideas of a research design that can be used to test the validity of this aspect and the hypothesis or hypotheses associated with it. By comparison, it would be illogical to discuss first your research design and then the theory – the validity of some aspect of which you are questioning. A reader must be able to follow the process of your thinking and of the development of your ideas.

Similarly, the parts of a thesis must form an integrated whole, which progresses in a logical sequence of information and ideas. To use the same analogy of the building of a house – the foundation (the introduction) must support the walls (the research), which in turn must support the roof (the discussion). Each part of your thesis, then, must follow logically from its predecessor and build upon it.

Importance

Sometimes, students do not fully appreciate the need for and importance of planning before they begin to write. The essence of good writing is to know what information and ideas you need to convey and the sequence in which you need to do so. Then, all that you need to do is to present the necessary information and ideas simply, clearly, and concisely.

Figures and tables

If something can be simply and concisely described in writing, then that is what should be done: no illustration is needed. On the other hand, a figure can be appropriately used to illustrate something that would otherwise be difficult to describe in writing, or to complement a written description. Similarly, the use of a table is appropriate if information can most efficiently be presented in this form.

As you plan the content of each part of your thesis, you should consider the advisability or necessity of the use of figures or tables. In particular, you must decide what it is that you want to illustrate or summarize, and whether this can be more effectively be achieved by the use of a figure or table than it can be in written form. Do not include any figure or table in your thesis that is not needed.

You should prepare any needed figures or tables in their final form as you write the relevant part of your thesis – ensuring that they comply with the specified editorial requirements. This is necessary to allow you to be sure that they clearly illustrate or present that which you intend and that appropriate reference to them is made in the text. In any event, designing and preparing figures and tables takes time, and so you do not want to be preparing them in a rush at the end.

Appendices

Appendices are not used to replace or complement a written explanation or description. Rather, they are used to present additional information to which a reader might want to refer (or perhaps simply material that is required by a department to be included in a thesis). For example, a questionnaire or other instrument used in research, or detailed data could be presented in the form of an appendix.

As you plan the content of each part of your thesis, you should consider the advisability or necessity of the inclusion of appendices. In particular, you consider what additional information it might be advisable or necessary to provide. Do not include any appendix that is not needed or specifically required. Students sometimes include a large number of unnecessary appendices in their theses, to which they do not refer in the text, and that seem to serve no useful purpose. In this case, an examiner is unlikely to look at the unnecessary appendices or, if he or she does, wonder why they were included.

As for figures and tables, you should prepare any needed or required appendices in their final form as you write the relevant part of your thesis – ensuring that they comply with the specified editorial requirements. Designing and preparing appendices takes time, and you do not want to be doing this in a rush at the end.

Computer printouts

A point to note is that it is not acceptable merely to photocopy computer printouts and to use these as figures, tables, or appendices. These usually do not well illustrate the point that you want to make or neatly summarize data or other information that you want to present. In any event, they will not be consistent with the specified editorial requirements.

▶ The introduction

It is important to understand that the introduction in a thesis is a literature review. Unlike a free-standing literature review, however, it ends with an outline research design that is intended to be used to investigate the research problem addressed and, where appropriate, the hypotheses to be tested.

From the perspective that it forms the foundation of your research, this is the most important part of your thesis. The research that you carry out is dependent on the ideas and reasoning presented here.

It follows that any flaw or weakness in the ideas that you present, or your reasoning, can later result in potentially serious problems. For this reason, ideally you should write the introduction in at least close to its final form before you begin to collect data.

In some instances, you might want to change your introduction after you have completed your research. For instance, you might want to add emphasis to some point or to further develop some issue. However, there should be no substantial change to the content of your introduction.

Time

The most time-consuming part of your thesis to write will be the introduction. Your first task is to seek out and obtain relevant sources. This takes time, particularly because some important sources that you need will inevitably not be available in the university library, and so must be found elsewhere. Then, you have to read analytically and critically the sources that you have obtained, and make notes. Finally, before you begin to write, you have to organize the material that you have found into a logical sequence of information and ideas.

Having planned your introduction, you will have to write a number of "working" drafts of it. You will also have to write at least one draft, and probably two, for your supervisor to read. It is important for you to do this, and to discuss your introduction with your supervisor as soon as possible. If you do not, there is a risk of you not detecting any possible problem that might later have a serious effect on your research. For example, you might have misunderstood some previous work in the area, or there might be a flaw in your reasoning.

In any event, collecting data takes considerable time. Consequently, if you have not completed your introduction in at least close to its final form before you begin to collect data, you are likely to find that it is impossible to do so while you are collecting data. This is especially so because you will also have coursework, personal, and probably employment commitments during this time. The result would be that you would have to write your thesis in its entirety after you have completed your data collection and analysis. You would, then, experience difficulty with completing your thesis before the due date for submission, and this is very likely to result in it being poorly written. More than one student has "fallen for this trap".

Structure

The structure of an introduction will vary somewhat with the nature of the research, development of the ideas involved, and personal preferences; but, in any event, it will progress in a logical sequence leading to an outline of the intended research and, where appropriate, the hypothesis or hypotheses to be tested. In the case of quantitative research that involves a single experiment or study, the main parts of the introduction will be

- an introduction to the area,
- definition of the research problem to be addressed,
- review of the relevant literature,
- definition of the research question to be investigated,
- theoretical hypothesis,
- outline research design that can be used, and
- research (or experimental) hypothesis to be tested.

Multiple hypotheses
When multiple hypotheses are to be tested, there will be some logical progression in the order in which they are developed and presented, and this must be readily evident. The evidence and reasoning leading to hypotheses must be developed as the introduction progresses. You cannot simply "tag on" your hypotheses at the end of your introduction.

Depending on the length of the introduction, at what points hypotheses were developed and their number, at the end of the introduction a reader can have difficulty with recalling exactly what hypotheses are involved and why. In such circumstances, it is advisable to include a section at the end of the introduction headed "Hypotheses" under which the hypotheses to be tested are given again. However, when this is done hypotheses should not be presented simply in the form of a list: some brief explanation of why the hypotheses given are to be tested should be given.

Multiple experiments or studies
If the research involves multiple experiments or studies, the introduction proper will not include the outline research designs or hypotheses involved. In this case, each experiment or study will be preceded by an introduction that summarizes important and specifically relevant material from the introduction proper, and that gives an outline research design and hypotheses to be tested in that experiment or study.

Headings

Typically, headings will be needed in the introduction to guide a reader. Those used and their number will vary with circumstances, and deciding on the headings to be included is a matter of judgement. For example, you might use headings such as "Theoretical Issues", "Research Approaches", "Measurement of the Dependent Variable", or "Research Design". Such headings should be part of the plan that you prepare for your introduction. A point to note, however, is that heading should be used judiciously. Numerous headings and sub-headings can sometimes merely add "clutter".

Aim of the research

Students sometimes notice in material that has been given to them a comment such as, "The aims and rationale of the research must be clear." As a result, on occasion they form the idea that they must include at the end of their introductions a section headed "Aims and Rationale" in which they describe why they intend to carry out the described research. While in some exceptional circumstances this might be necessary, in the vast majority of cases it is not. Rather, it is superfluous and wastes words.

It is always the case that research is carried out to address a research problem that is of some importance, and to investigate some research question with a view to finding a solution or partial solution to the research problem. The research problem and question will already have been presented earlier in the introduction, and so the aim of the research should be self-evident. When hypotheses are involved, the research will always be designed to test these. Therefore, it would be superfluous to comment that the aim of the research is to address the research problem, to investigate the research question, or to test the given hypotheses.

Qualitative research

Apart from those aspects relating to hypotheses, the introduction to a qualitative thesis does not differ from that of a quantitative thesis. Qualitative research might not involve the testing of hypotheses. On the other hand, although not in the form of a conventional hypothesis, if possible, the expected outcome of the research and the reasoning leading to this expectation should be given.

In any event, the introduction must end by giving a clear direction to the intended research. In particular, how an answer to the research question to be investigated will provide a solution or partial solution to the research problem being addressed must be clear.

▶ The research

Although the importance of the introduction has been stressed, this should not be taken to suggest that the research part of your thesis is not important: it is. The success of your thesis is largely determined by the validity of the research that you carried out. Therefore, you must present a clear and coherent account of your research.

Much of the content of this part of your thesis will be in the form of information. For example, it is here that you will present details of the sample used in your research and statistics that you calculated. However, ideas are also involved. Your description of the manipulation of an independent variable, for instance, represents your idea of how this could effectively be done. In qualitative research, this is where you will present ideas such as some theme or relationship that you detected in your research, and this again is an idea.

Time

Planning and writing the research part of your thesis is time-consuming; especially if it involves pilot or validation research, or multiple experiments or studies. In particular, care must be taken in planning this part of the thesis so that it forms a logical sequence of information and ideas that can readily be followed by a reader. Moreover, designing and preparing any necessary figures, tables, or appendices, takes time.

Structure

The structure of the research part of a thesis will vary with the nature of the investigation and with the number of experiments or studies involved. Put simply, however, this part of a thesis must be structured so that a reader can readily understand what was done and why, how the data were analysed and why they were analysed in this manner, and what was found.

Single experiment or study

Planning the research part of a thesis is straightforward when only a single experiment or study is involved. Nonetheless, care is needed. For instance, in some cases it might be advisable to include a description of the apparatus used and of the task that participants were required to perform under a heading such as "Apparatus and Experimental Tasks". Similarly, when reporting the results it might, for example, be advisable to include a section under a sub-heading such as "Preliminary Analysis" or "Data Transformation" in which the relevant analysis or data transformation is described.

Consistency

You must ensure that this part of the thesis is consistent with the introduction. For instance, you need to make sure that the detailed description of the research design given in this part is consistent with the outline design given in the introduction. A potential problem, which can have serious consequences, is differences in the wording of hypotheses in the introduction and the research part of the thesis. You must ensure that the wording of hypotheses is consistent.

Purpose

It is important to relate any data analysis used to the purpose of the research. This part of a thesis must not suggest that you carried out a "fishing expedition" or are simply trying to demonstrate your statistical expertise. The reason for, and relevance of, any analysis that you used must be readily apparent. Sometimes, this will be obvious and so not require comment. On the other hand, in some instances you will have to explain why you did what you did. For example, if you used any data transformation you would need to explain why you did so.

Hypothesis testing

When reporting the outcome of testing a research hypothesis, you must give the relevant descriptive and inferential statistics. Where appropriate, a figure or table may be included in this part of the thesis, but what it is intended to illustrate must be clearly indicated in the text. A point to note is that the inclusion of a statistical analysis or table as an appendix does not obviate the necessity of including a needed figure or table in the body of the thesis.

Multiple hypotheses
If multiple hypotheses were tested, particular care is needed when planning the structure of this part of the thesis. The hypotheses involved will have been presented in the introduction in some logical sequence. It follows that the outcome of testing them should appear in the same sequence in this part of the thesis. In any event, a reader will be referring back to the introduction, and he or she must readily be able to relate the hypotheses in both parts of the thesis.

Pilot or validation research

When pilot or validation research is involved, the research part of the thesis will include two sub-parts: the pilot or validation research and the research proper. In this case, each sub-part will have its own short introduction and a discussion (or perhaps a combined results and discussion). Planning each sub-part, therefore, essentially involves planning a separate small research report. However, the introduction will include only that material which is necessary to introduce the pilot or validation research, or the research proper, and will refer only briefly to relevant material that is included in the introduction of the thesis.

As soon as you have collected and analysed the relevant data, you will have to write the pilot or validation part of your thesis – in at least close to its final form – so that you can discuss the outcome with your supervisor. This is important because the research proper depends on the outcome of the pilot or validation experiment or study. Therefore, you must be confident of the outcome of any such experiment or study so that you can ensure that you do not encounter any problems with the research proper.

Multiple experiments or studies

If multiple experiments or studies are involved, planning the research part of the thesis will, in effect, involve planning several small research reports, each with its own introduction and discussion (or perhaps combined results and discussion). In this case, the outline research design adopted must be included in, and the hypotheses to be tested must be developed and given in, the introduction to each experiment or study.

You will have to write the resulting sub-parts of your thesis as you progress so that you can discuss the outcome of each experiment or study with your supervisor. This is necessary because each experiment or study (after the first) must follow logically from its predecessor. Later, when finalizing your thesis, you will probably make some changes to these parts. Nonetheless, it is of value to write them as you progress with your research.

Qualitative research

What is involved in planning the research part of a thesis that reports qualitative research will vary with the nature of the investigation. Reporting research of this type involves more of a narrative account of what was done and what was found than is the case in quantitative research. Planning this part of the thesis, therefore, is more of an art than a science. It remains, however, that the research must be reported in a logical sequence of information and ideas.

When writing this part of a qualitative thesis, it is important to consider the sub-headings that you use. These can greatly assist a reader to follow your account of what you did and of the data analyses that you employed. For instance, you might use a sub-heading such as "The sample" under which you record relevant demographic details, "Interviews" under which you record the relevant details of what happened, or "Preliminary Analysis" under which you discuss trends or relationships that become evident in the initial data analysis.

▶ The discussion

This part of the thesis is important because it is here that you present the ideas that you have developed as a result of the outcome of your research, and relate this to the information, ideas, and theory referred to in the introduction. In particular, it is here that you present your answer to the research question that you investigated, and your suggested solution or partial solution to the research problem addressed.

It is also here that you comment on implications of the outcome of your research and suggest possible future directions for investigation of the research problem. This allows for some creative speculation and theorizing, which you are likely to find both interesting and rewarding. However, you must support any ideas that you propose on the basis of evidence and sound, logical reasoning: you cannot simply offer "wild guesses". Being creative and speculative, therefore, require careful thought. This takes time and, at this stage, you are likely to be in a hurry to finish your thesis. Consequently, you will not be free to ponder *ad infinitum*.

Time

By comparison with the introduction, writing the discussion part of a thesis is not so time-consuming. You will already have sought out and read the relevant sources, and you will know the outcome of your research. On the other hand, you should not underestimate the time and effort involved. Too often, students write their discussions in a rush in order to have their theses completed by the due date for submission – with the result that they are poorly written. There has been more than one instance of a student having carried out a good piece of research, but not being awarded a good grade because he or she did not allow adequate time for writing the discussion.

Structure

Writing a good discussion requires care. You have to think carefully about the outcome of your research, and plan your discussion so that it forms a logical progression of information and ideas that can readily be followed by a reader. Put another way, each part of your discussion must lead logically to the next. In addition, this part of a thesis must follow logically from the introduction. Although it will vary, generally the structure of this part of a thesis will be in the form of the

- outcome of testing the research hypotheses,
- theoretical hypothesis,
- previous research findings and ideas,
- answer to the research question,
- proposed solution or partial solution to the research problem,
- possible alternative explanations of the outcome,
- possible weaknesses in the research, and
- suggested directions for future research.

In the case of qualitative research, the testing of hypotheses may not be involved. On the other hand, the discussion should begin with a summary of the findings of the research and, if an expected outcome was suggested in the introduction, how the findings relate to this should be discussed.

Important information, ideas, and theory included in the introduction should be referred to in the discussion. If they cannot be, then it would seem that they are not relevant and so should not have been included in the introduction. On the other hand, although it is sometimes acceptable – for instance, in the event of some unusual and unexpected finding – new material should not be introduced in the discussion. Any relevant information, ideas, or theory should have been included in the introduction.

Headings

Your discussion is likely to be quite lengthy and so, as for the introduction, it will no doubt be necessary to use headings to guide a reader. The number and nature of such headings will vary with the nature of your research and in particular of your discussion, and so is a matter of judgement. As for the introduction, headings should be used judiciously.

Consistency

Before you begin to write your discussion, you must read all of the preceding parts of your thesis that you have already written. It is particularly important that you read the introduction carefully, because you will have written this some time previously and you might well have forgotten some detail in it, or your thinking on some point might have changed in the intervening period. Therefore, if you are not careful, it is very easy to include something in your discussion that is not consistent with the material in your introduction.

A potential problem, which can have serious consequences, is differences in the wording of hypotheses in the introduction, the research parts of the thesis, and the discussion. In some instances, even small differences in wording can result in differences in hypotheses. Of course, you need to make sure that if you have reported in the research part of your thesis that a hypothesis was not supported, that you do not discuss it in the discussion on the basis that it was.

On one occasion, a student made the mistake of rewording a hypothesis by simply reversing the order of variables, so that the hypothesis proposed in the introduction and tested in the results section was the opposite to that discussed in the discussion. Such a mistake is easy to make in the pressure to complete the writing of a thesis. Another student, who apparently did not read her introduction before writing the discussion, argued that her findings were consistent with a theory that she had discussed in the introduction, when in fact her findings were not. Errors of this type can have serious consequence, and so you must take care to avoid them

Multiple hypotheses

When multiple research hypotheses have been tested, the order in which the outcome of testing them is reported can sometimes be problematic. There will have been some logical reason for presenting them in a given order in the introduction; and, ideally, this same sequence should have been used when reporting the outcome of testing them in the discussion. This makes it much easier for a reader to follow a thesis.

Often, however, one hypothesis is not supported while others were, or perhaps more than one was not supported. When this is so, it is usually preferable to report first the outcome of testing hypotheses that were supported. In any event, your interpretation of the outcome will determine some order. As a general principle, the most important findings should be reported first.

Confusion between hypotheses can easily result if care is not taken. For example, one student who had tested two hypotheses and found that only one was supported, apparently became confused and reported in his discussion that the hypothesis that was supported was not, and that that which was not was. This caused him some considerable difficulty with explaining the outcome of his research: obviously, his resulting interpretation of the outcome of his research was invalid. It also confused the examiners.

A point to note is that an examiner can find it to be very frustrating if it is necessary to refer back and forth between your introduction and your discussion when trying to follow how what you found relates to what you originally expected. If this is necessary, apart from making it difficult (if not impossible) for an examiner to follow your thesis, the resultant confusion suggests muddled thinking on your part. This problem is exacerbated if the sequence of testing hypotheses reported in the results section is different yet again. Such frustration and difficulty are not likely to result in a good grade being awarded to your thesis.

Multiple experiments or studies

If the research involved multiple experiments or studies, the outcome of each will have been discussed in the discussion section, or perhaps in a combined results and discussion section, of each. In this case, the discussion part of the thesis is generally described as a general discussion, in which the outcome of the series of experiments or studies involved is discussed in summary form. It remains, however, that it is here that the answer to the research question being invest-igated is given, and how this offers a solution or partial solution to the research problem addressed is proposed.

In the same way that the order of reporting the outcome of testing of multiple hypotheses can be problematic, the order of presenting the outcome of multiple experiments or studies can be similarly so. Again, there will have been some logical reason for carrying out the experiments or studies in the sequence in which this was done, and this should dictate the order in which the outcomes are reported. However, just as in a single experiment or study a hypothesis might not be supported, this sometimes also happens in the case of multiple experiments or studies. When this is so, care will need to be taken in the planning of the discussion so that a coherent account and inter-pretation of the outcome of the research is presented. In particular, the interrelationship between the experiments or studies and their outcomes must be made clear.

Qualitative research

When the research involved is of a qualitative nature, planning the discussion can be difficult. Typically, the discussion in a qualitative thesis is largely in the form of a narrative, and so its planning is more of an art than a science. This is especially so when, as is sometimes appropriate, a combined findings and discussion section is used, and so the findings must be concurrently interpreted and related to the research question and problem. In any event, you must plan your discussion so that it progresses in a logical sequence of information and ideas.

Although it is likely to be more in the form of a narrative than is found in a quantitative thesis, the discussion in a qualitative thesis may not be simply in the form of a "story" of what you did and found. It remains that you must relate your findings to information, ideas, and theory referred to in the introduction. In particular, you must relate your discussion to the research question that you investigated and so to the research problem. A thesis that is of a qualitative nature may not be simply descriptive in nature; it must at least attempt to explain the outcome of the research. In addition, you need to acknowledge any possible alternative explanations of your findings and any weaknesses in your research.

Ending

It is easy to overlook the need to plan an ending for a thesis. You need to understand that it is very unlikely that a reader will have read your thesis in "one sitting". It is more probable that he or she will read it as you will have written it, that is, in parts. In any event, it would be unreasonable to expect a reader to remember everything in your thesis. Therefore, you need to present a brief summary at the end of your discussion in which you bring together the key points, summarize your reasoning, and present your conclusions. In particular, you will have to restate the research problem that you addressed, briefly summarize the research that you carried out to investigate it and the outcome, and explain how your findings contribute to a solution or partial solution to the research problem. Achieving this will require careful planning.

▶ Abstract

When you have completed the writing of all else that is needed, it remains for you to write your abstract.[2] This is difficult, because in your abstract you will have to summarize a large volume of information and ideas.

You will previously have written abstracts for research reports, and so you will be familiar with what is required. Put simply, you have to summarize your research and its outcome in a limited number of words. In a conventional thesis the allowed length of an abstract is typically in the order of 250–300 words. On the other hand, in a thesis that is in the form of a journal article it might be limited to about 120–150 words. No doubt, you will have to write several drafts to comply with the allowed length.

▶ **Back-up**

While writing the parts of your thesis, you must consider the possibility of inadvertently deleting a file, a "computer crash", or in some other way losing work that you have written. There are various stories about people who did not do so. For instance, one masters student advertised in the press for the return of the only copy of her thesis, which had been in her car when it was stolen (she was not overly worried about the car), and one PhD student lost the only copy of his thesis when his home was engulfed in a bushfire. The point is, when writing any part of your thesis you must always keep at least one back-up copy in another secure location.

A back-up copy can be on paper, but this might result in problems. There is a story of a professor who, following a flood, was trying to retrieve a paper that he had written from under 1 metre of mud. Preferably, you should keep at least one copy in electronic form in another location so that, in the event of any mishap, you will not have to retype your work.

How often a back-up copy should be made is a matter of judgement. You need to consider how frequently you work on your thesis, and how much work you would need to rewrite in the event of a mishap. For example, if you work on your thesis on one day per week, you would be wise to make a weekly back-up. By comparison, during a concentrated period of writing over some days, you might need to make a back-up copy every day.

Another consideration is how many back-up copies you want to keep, and for how long. For example, you might decide to keep a copy of each draft that you write, and so you will have a number of back-up files. Alternatively, you might decide to keep only a back-up of the current draft. In any event, it is advisable to label clearly each back-up file so that it can readily be identified. You might, for instance, label files as "Draft 1" and so on. It is a good idea to include the date on which a draft is written – not the date on which it was saved, which might be different. This will allow you to identify readily your most recent draft.

▶ Some advice on writing

The key to good writing is to know what you want to convey to the reader, and to communicate this in such a manner that a reader can readily understand the information and ideas involved. This, of course, requires writing in a scholarly manner (i.e., the manner in which an educated person would write).

You will already be familiar with the requirements of writing in psychology, and you will have had experience with writing papers such as essays and research reports. Therefore, you should have no particular difficulty (other than that writing is always hard work and takes longer than you anticipate) with writing your thesis. For this reason, and because it is beyond the scope of this book, no attempt has been made here to give you any specific advice or guidance on writing. There are texts that have been written on writing in psychology. If need be, you should refer to one of these texts for guidance.

Perhaps the best advice that can be offered to you is to begin writing your thesis as early as possible and to plan adequate time for the writing of its parts. Do not forget to allow time for the writing of a number of working drafts, and probably two drafts for your supervisor.

Like everyone else, you will encounter periods of "writers' block". You might have allocated a particular day to writing some part of your thesis; but, on that day, you find that you simply cannot write. This is always frustrating and, particularly if you are behind schedule, it can result in some anxiety. When you find that you cannot write, you are best advised to set the task aside. Do something that is less demanding on your creativity. For example, you might do some work on the reference list, or on some figures or tables that you need. Of course, you will, then, later need to "catch up" with your planned writing timetable.

11 Drafts and Editing

You will already be familiar with the need for writing and editing of drafts of papers such as essays and research reports. Similarly, you will have to write and edit drafts of your thesis. Most of those that you write will be for your own purposes and these can be described as "working drafts". However, you will also submit drafts to your supervisor for comment, and these must be distinguished from your working drafts.

▶ First working draft

When you write the first working draft of any part of your thesis, you should not be concerned with grammar, spelling, punctuation, and editorial style. Rather, you should concentrate on "getting your ideas onto paper".

Writing and thinking are inextricably linked. Before you begin to write, you will have decided on the information and ideas that you want to communicate, and the sequence in which you intend to present them. However, as you write you will find that the part of your thesis that you are working on "develops". Consequently, you may decide that you want to modify your original plan for the structure of the part of the thesis involved. A common experience is that, although it seemed to be most appropriate when planning, it becomes apparent when writing that some sequence of information and ideas is not ideal. For instance, you might have planned a sequence of A, B, C, and D; but, as you write, you decide that a better sequence would be A, C, B, and D. If this were to happen, you should change your planned sequence.

As an example, when planning the introduction you might have decided that you should discuss first some relevant theory and then the research methods that have commonly been used in investigations of the research problem. However, when you write your first working draft, you might change your mind on the grounds that you think that the research methods used have influenced the development of the theory involved. Put another way, you might think that the paradigm adopted has influenced the development of the theory. Therefore, you might decide to discuss first the research methods used, or paradigm adopted, and then the theory.

It is important for you to understand that there is no one-perfect way to write any part of your thesis: any two people would write it differently, and no doubt you will be able to see more than one way to write any part. What matters is that you present the relevant information and ideas in a rational sequence, and that you develop your ideas on the basis of sound evidence and logical reasoning.

▶ Headings and pagination

Use appropriate headings and, where applicable, sub-headings in drafts, as you would do in the final version of your thesis. You will have decided on these when planning the part of your thesis that you are writing, and using them will help you to follow your plan, and so the sequence of ideas involved. In addition, they provide a guide that will help your supervisor to follow the progression of information, ideas, and reasoning involved in your drafts. They are also helpful to your supervisor when making comments: they allow for ready reference to a specific section. For the same reason, you should ensure that your draft is paginated.

▶ Editing

Having written the first working draft of a part of your thesis, you then need to edit it. There are three levels of editing, each of which is for a particular purpose. These can be described as editing for content, editing for consistency, and editing for detail. The first two can be carried out concurrently, but when doing so care is needed. The third level includes editing for (a) length, (b) grammar, spelling, and punctuation, (c) style and polish, and (d) editorial style. These levels of sub-editing should be carried out consecutively.

Working drafts need only be edited for content and consistency. Drafts submitted to your supervisor, however, must be edited at all levels; as, of course, eventually must be the thesis in its entirety.

The advice on editing offered here is based on a thesis written on quantitative research; but, in principle, it applies equally to qualitative research. The only real difference is that sometimes a qualitative thesis is structured so that the results and discussion are partly or entirely combined. In this case, the editing involved will be a combination of that needed for the research section together with that for the editing of the discussion section of a quantitative thesis.

▶ Editing for content

Having written the first working draft of any part of your thesis, you should set it aside for a few days and forget about it. Then, you should edit it for content. This means that you should read your draft as you would read any book or article: you should read it analytically and critically.

Check that you have supported all assertions and that the evidence and reasoning upon which you have made them are valid. In particular, ensure that you have developed any ideas that you propose by a process of logical reasoning based on sound evidence. Also, ensure that the development of your ideas follows the logical sequence of presenting first the relevant information, idea(s), or theory, and then developing your idea. Do not fall into the trap of "upside down" reasoning.

Make sure that everything that you have written is relevant and contributes to your argument, and that you have made clear the reason for including any information or idea. If anything included is irrelevant or not needed, it must be deleted.

Editing for content also involves checking for redundancy. Look for any unnecessary repetition. Sometimes, such repetition is not immediately obvious, usually because the same information or idea is given more than once, but in different wording.

The introduction

When editing a draft of the introduction, check that the ideas that you present follow one another in a logical sequence: each should build upon the ideas that you have already developed. In particular, make sure that you have clearly identified and defined the research problem addressed, and the research question to be investigated. Where appropriate, check that you have developed the theoretical and research hypotheses on the basis of logical reasoning, and that these are worded clearly and concisely. Finally, make sure that you have clearly and concisely described your outline research design and that this description can readily be related to the research hypotheses that you intend to test.

Writing the introduction in parts

If you are adopting book format for your thesis and the introduction is to include two or more chapters, you will write and edit these separately. In this case, editing of the individual chapters does not differ from that described above. When you have completed the writing and editing of the individual chapters, however, you must then edit them as a single entity: together, they form your introduction.

The research

For research involving a single experiment or study, the research part of your thesis will commonly include two sections: the method and the results sections. Usually, the method section is written first. In any event, you will write each of these sections separately, and so you will have to edit these drafts separately – while bearing in mind the intimate relationship between them.

Editing the method section is usually straightforward. All that you need to do is to ensure that you have given the necessary details of the participants, respondents, or subjects involved, and that you have described clearly and concisely any apparatus or materials used and the procedure that you followed.

When editing the results section, you must ensure that a reader can understand the purpose of any analysis that you used and, where more than one is involved, the logic underlying the sequence of the analyses involved. For example, if you used a data transformation, and then an analysis of variance followed by post hoc analyses, the reason why you did so must be made clear, and the analyses used and their outcome must be reported in the sequence in which they were carried out.

Multiple hypotheses

If multiple hypotheses were tested, you will need to make sure that you report these in a logical sequence, ideally in the order in which they were developed and presented in the introduction. In any event, you must ensure that a reader can readily relate the hypotheses given in the introduction to your reported testing of them in the results section.

Multiple experiments or studies

When pilot or validation research and/or multiple experiments or studies are involved, you will write drafts of each of these subsections of your thesis as you progress. Therefore, you will find it necessary to edit drafts of each of these sub-sections individually. What is involved in this does not differ markedly from the editing of the research part of a thesis that reports only one experiment or study. The only real difference is that the pilot or validation research and each experiment or study included in the research proper will have its own introduction and discussion (or perhaps a combined results and discussion section). It is, therefore, necessary to ensure that each of these introductions includes a clear and concise outline description of the research design adopted. Where appropriate, you must ensure that the hypotheses to be tested are well developed and clearly and concisely stated in the introduction to the sub-section. You must also ensure that a reader can readily relate the hypotheses involved to the research design that you used.

The discussion

Editing the discussion is similar to editing the introduction. Like the introduction, the discussion is essentially a literature review, but one that includes the outcome of your research and its interpretation. Therefore, you should check that the ideas that you present follow one another in a logical sequence, and that each should build upon the ideas that you have already developed.

Because of the inevitable interval of time that occurs between the writing of the introduction and of the discussion, it is particularly important that you ensure that the ideas in the latter follow logically from and build upon those presented in the former. Immediately before editing your discussion, therefore, you should again read your introduction.

The first point that you should check is that, where appropriate, you have correctly reported the outcome of the testing of your research hypotheses. In any event, you must ensure that you have correctly interpreted the findings of your research. You should then ensure that you have discussed your findings in relation to the research question being investigated, and that you have at least attempted to offer an answer to this. Then you should check that you have related the findings of your research to the research problem being addressed. Where appropriate, this will include checking that you have related your findings to the theoretical hypothesis given in the introduction. In particular, you need to ensure that you have at least attempted to propose a solution or partial solution to the research problem being addressed, and discussed the implications of your findings.

At a general level, you should check that you have related your findings to the information, ideas, and theory referred to in the introduction. If they are relevant to the research problem being addressed, you should be able to do this. You should also check that you have not introduced any new material, unless there is some particular reason for doing so.

Having done all else, you should ensure that you have discussed any possible alternative explanations of the outcome and any possible weaknesses in the research. In addition, you should ensure that you have suggested appropriate directions for future research.

Finally, you need to make sure that you have ended your discussion with a clear and concise summary of your research.

Pilot or validation research

When pilot research was conducted for some specific purpose, or validation research, you need to check that you have referred appropriately to the outcome. Commonly, this will involve simply discussing the outcome in terms of the purpose of this subsidiary research. It is usually necessary to do this before, or concurrently with, presenting the outcome of the research proper.

Multiple experiments or studies

If the research that you are reporting involved multiple experiments or studies, you will have to take care when editing the discussion. In this situation, the discussion can easily become very complicated and confusing. You will therefore, need to ensure that you have presented a coherent account of the research being reported. In particular, you need to check that you have made clear the progression of your research, and how the outcome of each experiment or study led logically to the next.

► A second opinion

A problem that you will find with editing your work is that you know what you are trying to convey, and commonly you will believe that you have clearly done so – even if you have not. Moreover, especially after writing and editing several drafts of a given part of your thesis, your perception of what you have written can become "clouded". Every author experiences these problems from time to time. That is why you must leave a draft aside for a few days before editing it – hopefully with a "fresh perspective".

When you have reached a point at which you think your draft of a part of your thesis is close to the final version, it is a good idea to have someone else read it. Do not wait until your supervisor does so. Any draft of a part of your thesis that you submit to your supervisor should be as close as possible to the final version because this will ultimately save time. In any event, there will be some limit on the number of drafts that your supervisor can or may read.

At this point, it is not essential that a reader can fully understand what you have written. Rather, what you need to know is that someone else, who is not familiar with your work, can follow your draft. If it is well written, even someone who is not familiar with psychology should be able to follow it, although perhaps with some difficulty. Therefore, if you ask someone else to read a draft, and that person cannot follow some content, it is likely that you will need to make some change(s).

► Editing for consistency

The purpose of editing for consistency is to ensure that there are no internal inconsistencies within or between parts of your thesis. For example, if you were to argue in an early part of the introduction that some previous research finding clearly shows something, later in the introduction you cannot argue that it shows the opposite. Similarly, you obviously cannot report in the results section that a hypothesis was not supported, and then in the discussion section discuss it as though it was.

A particular point to bear in mind when editing is that, because you will write your thesis in parts you will edit it in parts, you must ensure that it is internally consistent. This means that you must consider not only the content of the part that you are editing, but also that of the earlier part(s) that you have already written. A particular point to check is the wording, and where multiple hypotheses are involved the sequence, of hypotheses in the introduction, results, and discussion sections.

If you have adopted a book format for your thesis, it is particularly important to edit each chapter (after the first) for consistency with its predecessor. You will have written the chapters that comprise the introduction individually over some time, and so it is easy to overlook the presence of some inadvertent inconsistency.

▶ Making changes

Invariably, when you edit the first working draft of any part of your thesis for content and consistency, you will find flaws or weaknesses. Your task, then, is to rectify these. This will mean that you have to rewrite your first draft.

When you have written your second working draft, you should repeat this process. Again, leave it aside for a few days and then edit it for content and consistency. When you do so, it is most likely that you will still find some flaws or weaknesses in your work. In some instances, these might have resulted from changes that you made to your first draft. For example, you might have inserted a sentence or paragraph to clarify some point; but on reading the material in its entirety, you find that you have not effectively done so, or that the sentence or paragraph does not fit into the logical sequence of thought involved. Having detected the inevitable flaws and weaknesses, you will have to rectify them by writing a further draft. You will have to repeat this process of writing and editing until you are satisfied with what you have written.

▶ Editing for detail

When you are satisfied with the content of the part of your thesis that you are writing, with its internal consistency, and with its consistency with other parts of the thesis, you need to edit it for detail.

Length

You will have considered the overall length of your thesis and of its parts when planning it, and you will have allotted "space" to each part. All that you can do, therefore, is to work on this allotment for each part when editing it for length. Of course, you do not have to comply strictly with the word limit that you initially set for any given part of your thesis. On the other hand, if you exceed it you need to consider the effect on the length that you have allowed for later parts. In any event, a draft of any part of your thesis should be as short as possible.

When editing for length, delete anything that is not needed. Although you will have considered the relevance of material when editing for content, you might find it necessary to delete some to reduce the length of a draft. This can be a very difficult decision. You will have convinced yourself that everything that you have included is important. Nonetheless, it is always possible that something can be deleted, or that the discussion of some point can be abbreviated. In particular, look for any redundancy.

Grammar, spelling, and punctuation

You must edit the part of the thesis that you have written for grammar, spelling, and punctuation. No doubt, your first step will be to use a grammar and spelling checker, but these are not infallible. Often, they do not detect spelling or typing errors, and the grammatical and punctuation corrections suggested can sometimes be misleading. In addition, they do not detect incorrect word use. For example, a spelling checker will not detect the difference between "their" and "there", or "dependent" and "dependant". Similarly, typing errors such as "form" instead of "from" will not be detected.

Before you use a grammar and spelling checker, make sure that you have set it to the language in which you are writing: most provide this option. In particular, check that you are using Standard English spelling (unless you are writing in America). There is some difference between countries in spelling, and the best advice is to use British spelling for Standard English. Also, if the option is available, set your grammar and spelling checker to "Formal English". This should allow you to detect any contractions or colloquialisms that you might inadvertently have used.

In the end, you will have to read your draft carefully to check for grammar, spelling, and punctuation. If you are in doubt, consult a suitable dictionary or a book on English usage.

Style and polish

When you are satisfied with all else, you need to edit the part of your thesis that you have written for style. A thesis must be written in a scholarly manner; that is, in the manner in which an educated person would write. Apart from being correct in regard to grammar, spelling, and punctuation, this means that word use must be correct, that sentences and paragraphs must be well structured, and that each paragraph leads to the next.

In addition, a thesis should be written in a "polished" manner. For example, long and convoluted sentences should not be used. On the other hand, a series of short abrupt sentences does not read well. The same applies to paragraphs. Prose has rhythm, and writing should read smoothly.

Editorial style

Finally, you must edit your draft for editorial style. You will have been given some editorial style that you are required to follow. Most commonly, this will be the style recommended in the *Publication Manual of the American Psychological Society*. Editorial style is discussed in Chapter 12.

▶ Supervisors' drafts

The purpose of submitting a draft of a part of your thesis to your supervisor is to allow him or her to comment on your work and to suggest how you might make improvements. However, you should understand that there is no point in presenting your supervisor with a draft of a part of your thesis and asking something like, "Is this right?" If you have devoted adequate care to the planning of the part of your thesis involved, and have written and edited a number of working drafts of it, then it should "work". Therefore, you should expect your supervisor to reply by saying something like, "It is quite acceptable, but I would have written it differently."

A point that students sometimes overlook is that academics have responsibilities other than supervising their individual work. Do not expect your supervisor to be able to "drop everything" to read and comment upon your drafts. Rather, you should give a draft to your supervisor and arrange a meeting at some future time at which to discuss it.

After a supervisor has read a student's draft, and typically made notes on it, he or she will discuss the draft with the student. Sometimes, a supervisor will return the student's work at a meeting at which the draft is discussed. At other times, a supervisor might prefer first to return the annotated draft to the student for his or her consideration before discussing it. This allows students time to consider their supervisor's written comments before discussing their draft in person.

Quality of drafts

When you submit the first draft of any part of your thesis to your supervisor, you are presenting your ideas. Therefore, it is very important that you clearly develop, support, and communicate these. To achieve this, the content of your first draft must be well organized so that the logical progression of your thinking and reasoning is clear. Similarly, sentences and paragraphs must be well constructed so that your ideas are readily evident.

Use appropriate headings and, where applicable, sub-headings in drafts, as you would do in the final version of your thesis. These provide a guide that will help your supervisor to follow the progression of information, ideas, and reasoning involved. In addition, they are helpful to your supervisor when making comments on a draft: They allow for ready reference to a specific section. For the same reason, you should ensure that your draft is paginated.

Drafts that you submit to your supervisor should be well written and presented so that he or she can concentrate on the ideas involved, and not be distracted by flaws such as errors in grammar, spelling, punctuation, or editorial style. If a first draft is well written, and the student's supervisor can readily follow the reasoning involved and understand the ideas presented, he or she will be able to give the student appropriate advice. The supervisor might, for example, suggest that some idea should be more fully developed, that some material should be reorganized, or perhaps that a stronger argument is needed to support some assertion.

If a first draft is poorly written, the student's supervisor will have difficulty with following the reasoning involved and understanding the ideas presented. Consequently, it would be very difficult to give the student appropriate advice. A supervisor cannot "think for" a student. All that can really be done, therefore, is to make comments of a very general nature and suggest that the student starts again from virtually the beginning.

Your aim should be to submit to your supervisor a first draft that is as close as possible to the final version. Ideally, your first draft should be your last; but, in practice, this is unlikely. Typically, your supervisor will detect some problems and will make some suggestions, and so you will need to make changes and submit a second draft. With minor amendments, this should result in the final version of the part of your thesis involved.

Number of drafts

There will be some limit on the number of drafts that you may submit to your supervisor. In part, this will be determined simply by the time available, but it is likely that it will also be determined by department policy. For example, a department might set a limit of two drafts. Such a restriction is intended to ensure that all students are treated equally. In addition, it is the policy in some departments that a supervisor is not permitted to read a draft of the discussion. This restriction is intended to give students the opportunity to express their ideas freely, without being influenced by their supervisors.

Submission of drafts of parts

You should progressively submit drafts of parts of your thesis to your supervisor as you complete them. This allows you to take advantage of your supervisor's comments and to rectify any problems that might affect the writing of later parts. It also helps you to discipline your writing in terms of time and to monitor its progress.

If your thesis is to be presented in book format, and the introduction comprises two or more chapters, it is possible to submit drafts of each chapter separately to your supervisor. In the end, however, your supervisor must be able to read and consider your introduction in its entirety before he or she can give you fully appropriate feedback. This means that your supervisor cannot give you adequate comments until he or she has read all of the chapters that comprise the introduction.

Pilot or validation research

In the case of a research project that involves pilot research that is to be reported separately, or validation research, it is important to ensure that your supervisor has read and commented upon a draft of this research in its entirety before you proceed. This is necessary to ensure that there is no undetected flaw or weakness in the pilot or validation research that could lead to a problem in the research proper.

Multiple experiments or studies

When a research project involves multiple experiments or studies, you should submit a draft of each in its entirety to your supervisor, and discuss it with him or her before you proceed. Each experiment or study must lead logically to the next. Therefore, any undetected flaw or weakness in an experiment or study is likely to result in a problem in its successor.

Drafts of parts

Because you will submit drafts of parts of your thesis over a period, it will be difficult for your supervisor to "keep track" of your work. This is particularly so because academics usually supervise more than one student, and typically in research of a similar nature. Therefore, when submitting a draft of a part of your thesis for comment, you should provide copies of the final versions of previous parts that you have written. This will allow your supervisor to refer back to earlier material. For example, when you submit a draft of the results section, your supervisor will need to be able to refer back to the introduction section to relate the hypotheses given there to the analysis presented in the results section.

Comments on drafts

When reading the first draft of any part of a thesis, a supervisor's aim is to detect any problems and to bring these to the student's attention so that they can be rectified. In particular, a supervisor will be concentrating on the ideas involved, and how these have been developed and supported.

A point that students sometimes do not understand is that the advice offered on drafts of parts of a thesis by their supervisors will essentially be directed only to content. It is likely that, where appropriate, a supervisor will also make comment on matters such as sentence and paragraph structure, grammar, spelling, and punctuation, or editorial style. However, although a supervisor might draw a student's attention to flaws or weaknesses in these areas, and perhaps point out examples, he or she will not attempt to detect all of them, or to correct them. The responsibility for accuracy in these areas rests with the *student*.

Similarly, when reading a draft of the part of a thesis in which data analyses are reported, a supervisor will consider the purpose for any analysis, the logic and reasoning involved, and perhaps whether or not the results of analyses appear to be reasonable. Again, however, responsibility for accuracy of analyses rests with the *student*.

Sometimes, students are concerned because their supervisors have made a large number of written comments on their draft, which can be very disheartening. If this were to happen to you, you should pause, remember that your supervisor is trying to help you, and consider calmly the nature of the comments made. Presuming that you have devoted adequate time and effort to your work, you will usually find that most of the comments are of a minor nature. Moreover, often some will duplicate one another. For example, you might have repeatedly made some minor error and your supervisor has indicated many of these errors in an automatic manner. As a result, you might find that relatively few comments of a major nature have been made. Typically, when you discuss your draft with your supervisor in person, you will find that "things are not as bad" as they initially seemed to be.

On the other hand, sometimes students are concerned because there are relatively few written comments on their drafts. This can arise because there is little upon which to comment, or because the supervisor prefers to discuss the details of his or her observations on the draft in person. In this case, any concern that the student has can be resolved at a meeting with the supervisor.

The important point to make here is that you should not rely simply on written comments on a draft of any part of your thesis. You need to discuss your draft in person with your supervisor. This allows you to clarify any issues about which you are uncertain.

Another possible problem that can arise is that sometimes students are concerned because they think that their supervisors have made too many comments on their drafts that are negative, and too few that are positive. In this situation, the point to understand is that all supervisors will try to help their students to rectify any problems with their work. Therefore, where any flaws or weaknesses are detected, supervisors will point them out to students and try to help them to rectify the problem. Omitting to point out flaws and weaknesses, and emphasizing the good points in a draft, might result in a student have a "warm feeling", but the student might not have the same reaction when an examiner subsequently detects the flaws and weaknesses involved that have not been rectified. It is, therefore, important to accept critical comments as they are intended – that is, to help you.

▶ Revising the first draft

Your supervisor cannot "write your thesis for you". All that he or she can do is to point out any apparent flaws or weaknesses in your work, and suggest how you might improve it. Therefore, after you have discussed the first draft of a part of your thesis with your supervisor, you will need to consider carefully any issues raised and any suggestions that he or she has made. Then, you will have to rewrite, edit, and revise the part of your thesis involved until you are satisfied with what you have written. At this point, you can submit the second draft to your supervisor.

▶ The second supervisor's drafts

Because you will have considered any issues raised and any suggestions that he or she made on your first draft, and made any necessary changes to it before you submit your second, your supervisor will not expect to find any major problems in it. Rather, he or she will expect to be making suggestions of only a minor nature so that you can write the final version. It follows that the second draft that you submit to your supervisor should be in very close to the final form of that part of your thesis. After you have discussed the second draft with your supervisor, you should be in a position to make any minor changes needed and so produce the final version of that part of your thesis.

When you write the final version of any part of your thesis, you will have to edit it very carefully. A point that you should understand is that your supervisor will not have tried to detect every mistake or flaw in your work. It is not a supervisor's role to act as your editor or proofreader: responsibility for the content of your thesis rests with *you*.

▶ Some words of advice

You might well consider that writing and editing drafts of parts of your thesis is rather tedious, time-consuming, and frustrating. In this, you will not be alone. Writing is hard work! No one can write a first draft of any lengthy document that is completely satisfactory and so is, in effect, the final version. Everyone who writes a first draft of anything can, on later reading it, see possible changes that will result in improvements, and detect the mistakes that humans make. It is, of course, to be expected that subsequent drafts will include fewer flaws until, eventually, the final draft is "as good as possible". How many drafts are needed to arrive at this point will vary, but a number will be involved. You might like to consider that well-known authors of popular novels report that they write numerous drafts of their manuscripts – 15 is about the commonly reported number. If this is necessary when writing fiction, there is obviously a need to write numerous drafts of technical and scientific documents to ensure that they are well written – so that they effectively and accurately convey the necessary information and ideas.

The time and effort that you devote to the writing of your thesis will bring rewards. A copy of the thesis that you submit will be held in the university library indefinitely, where it will be accessible to anyone who wants to read it. A well-written thesis, therefore, will reflect favourably on you in the future. In any event, because you will justifiably take some pride in your work, you will want your thesis to be well written.

12 Finalizing the Thesis

When you have finished writing the parts that comprise the body of your thesis, you have to add the reference list, any needed or required appendices, and the preliminary pages. Before doing this, however, you need to check the presentation and other requirements of the department and university in which you are studying.

▶ Editorial style

You will have been advised of the editorial style that you are required to use in your thesis. Most commonly, this will be the editorial style recommended in the *Publication Manual of the American Psychological Association*. There is nothing "sacred" about this editorial style: it was not engraved on stone and given to Moses. There are other editorial styles. On the other hand, the APA editorial style is probably the most widely used in psychology. For convenience, therefore, this style has often been adopted by psychology departments. However, there are some aspects of the APA editorial style that you need to understand.

Any editorial style is simply a set of guidelines to ensure consistency in regard to matters such as spelling and punctuation, and in the presenting of material such as statistics, figures, and tables. It also includes guidance on matters such as spacing of text, and margins.

An important point to understand is that the *APA Manual* was published as a style guide for authors submitting manuscripts to APA journals. A thesis is a document in its final form, not a manuscript. This is recognized in the *APA Manual*, in which it is pointed out that variations from the style recommendations given in the manual are "not only permissible but desirable" in theses. Appendix A gives the editorial style requirements suggested in this book for theses, which incorporate recommended options in and deviations from the *APA Manual*. However, you will need to check for any particular requirements of the department in which you are studying. These take precedence and may differ in some instances from the requirements and guidance given in this chapter and Appendix A.

▶ The body of the thesis

No doubt, when writing the parts of your thesis you created separate computer files for each. If so, the first step in finalizing your thesis is to combine these into a single file, beginning with the introduction and ending with the discussion. The next step is to check that you have complied with the necessary editorial style requirements. You should have already checked the individual parts of your thesis when you prepared the final versions of them. Nonetheless, it is advisable to make a final check at this point. Appendix A and the following notes have been provided to assist you with this.

Running head

In books and published journal articles, a running head typically appears in the top margin of the page. Commonly, a running head is not used in a thesis, but if one is used it should be similarly positioned in the top margin and at the left of the page.

Margins

Both the top and bottom margins on a page should be about 35 mm. The right-side margin should also be about 35 mm, but the left-side margin is usually about 45 mm. These margins are designed to allow for trimming when binding professionally, which will result in a finished margin of a slightly lesser size. If the thesis is not to be professionally bound, the size of margins may be reduced slightly. However, it remains that the left margin must be larger than the right margin. Regardless of the form of binding used, some allowance must be made so that there is a clear margin on the left of the page. For visual appearance, this should be approximately equal to the right margin.

Spacing

Text is usually double spaced, but quadruple spacing should be left before a heading, and before and after a figure or table if it is incorporated with text on a page. Further recommendations on spacing are given in Appendix A.

As in most books, additional space is not left between paragraphs. To show that a new paragraph has started, the first line of each paragraph is indented by seven spaces. An exception to this is that there is no need to indent the first sentence in the introduction or the first sentence immediately following a heading or sub-heading – obviously, a new paragraph begins at this point.

Headings and sub-headings

The *APA Publication Manual* gives five levels of headings, and these provide a convenient format to use for headings and sub-headings in a thesis. The typing format for these five heading levels is shown in Box 1.

Box 1   Typing format for headings and sub-headings

Typing format	Level
CENTRED UPPER CASE	5
Centred Upper Case and Lower Case	1
Centred Upper Case and Lower Case	2
Flush Left Upper Case and Lower Case	3
Indented lower case.	4

Notes:
1. The Level 4 heading is a paragraph heading. It ends with a full stop, and the text of the paragraph begins two spaces after the full stop, on the same line.

▶ Report format

For a thesis involving only a single experiment or study, and which is presented in a research report format, only two levels of headings would usually be needed. These are illustrated in Box 2. If a third level is needed, a Level 4 (i.e., paragraph headings) could be used.

Box 2   Levels of headings for a thesis involving only a single experiment or study

		Level
	Method	1
Participants		3
Apparatus		3
Procedure		3
	Results	1
	Discussion	1
	References	1
	Appendices	1

Notes:
1. The introduction is not headed.
2. Any sub-headings used in the introduction may take the form of a Level 3 heading, and any lower level heading the form of Level 4 heading.

If the thesis involves multiple experiments or studies and is presented in a research report format, three levels of headings will be needed. Again, however, it is possible that a fourth level might be needed, in which case a Level 4 (i.e., paragraph headings) could be used. The three levels of headings that would usually be needed in such a thesis are illustrated in Box 3.

Book format
When a thesis is presented in book format, the chapter label should be typed as a Level 5 heading (e.g., "**CHAPTER 1**"), about 60 mm from the top of the page. This is done for visual effect, and to give a clear indication that a new chapter is beginning. The chapter title is then typed under this as a Level 1 heading (e.g., "**Research Approaches**"). Within the chapter, appropriate heading levels may then be used as needed. For example, if the chapter reported the outcome of a single experiment, two levels of headings (Levels 1 and 3) should suffice. (See the example headings for a thesis involving a single experiment that are shown in Box 2.)

Box 3   Levels of headings for a thesis involving multiple experiments or studies

		Level
	Experiment 1	1
	Method	2
Participants		3
Apparatus		3
Procedure		3
	Results	2
	Discussion	2
	Experiment 2	1
	Method	2
Participants		3
Apparatus		3
Procedure		3
	Results	2
	Discussion	2
	General discussion	1
	References	1
	Appendices	1

Note: The introduction to the thesis is not headed.

▶ Figures and tables

You should already have prepared any necessary figures and tables when writing the relevant parts of your thesis. At this point, you should check that each figure or table is appropriately referred to in the text, and is correctly numbered. It is also advisable to make a final check to ensure that figures and tables clearly illustrate the point(s) that you want to make, and that they comply with the necessary editorial style requirements. Finally, check that both axes of figures are labelled with the appropriate units and that any abbreviations or symbols used in figures or tables are consistent with those used in any other figures or tables in your thesis.

Numbering

Both figures and tables are numbered consecutively (but separately). In the case of multiple experiments or studies, numbering begins anew in each.

Figures

Figures should be positioned on the page centrally within the left and right margins. If a figure is presented on a page together with text, quadruple spacing should be left above and below the figure to clearly separate it from the text. If no text is included on the page, the top of the figure should be 35 mm from the top of the page.

Captions are typed under the figure and are left justified. The word *"Figure"* and the figure number are typed in italics, and the number is followed by a full stop. This is followed by the caption, which is typed in the same typeface as used in the text. A capital (upper-case) letter is used only for the first word in the caption.

Tables

Tables should be positioned on a page in the same manner as figures. However, the table title is typed 35 mm from the top of the page. The word "Table" is aligned with the left margin, and together with the table number is typed in the same typeface as the text. The table title is typed in italics two spaces under this, and aligned with the left margin. Capital (upper-case) letters are used for all principal words in the title

Landscape orientation

If necessary, figures and tables may be presented in landscape orientation. However, the page is paginated in portrait orientation. When presented in landscape orientation, figures and tables are centred between the normal top and bottom margins of the page. The top of the figure or the title of the table should be positioned at what would normally be the left margin of the page.

Paginating

To add a page number to a figure or a table in landscape format, it is usually necessary to print the required number and then to literally "cut and paste" it onto the figure or table, and then to photocopy it. Handwriting is not acceptable.

Inserting

If you are presenting figures or tables on pages without text, you will now have to decide where these are to be inserted into the thesis. A figure or table should appear as soon as possible after the first reference to it. You will have to use a "forced page break" to create blank pages in the appropriate places in your thesis, into which you can insert the necessary figures or tables. When doing this, always put the page break at the end of an existing page. Failure to do so can result in unwanted space on a page.

▶ Pagination

Having created a composite file of the body of your thesis, and if necessary inserted any blank pages to allow for insertion of figures or tables, you will have a file that will have been automatically paginated. However, there are some aspects of pagination to which you need to attend.

Pages on which figures or tables are presented are paginated in the same manner and in the same sequence as pages of text. An exception is that if a figure is in the form of a photograph or other illustration on which it is not practical to type, it may be not paginated.

Usually, the first page of the introduction is not paginated. For a thesis in book format, the first page of each chapter should be paginated at the bottom centre of the page or not paginated. Therefore, the normal pagination at the top right-hand corner should be deleted and, if appropriate, the page should be paginated at the bottom centre. To achieve this, you might find it necessary to create a separate (non-paginated) file for the first page of the introduction or each chapter and then to print each of these and replace the relevant page in the document with the new page.

▶ Reference list

Preparing a list of the publication details of sources to which you have referred in your thesis is straightforward. However, before finalizing it, you need to check that every source cited in the text is included in the reference list, and that you have not included any publication in the reference list that is not cited in the text. When you have done this, you need to check that you have included all of the necessary publication details and that you have complied with the necessary editorial style requirements.

Note that the reference list is headed "References" and that a hanging indent is used. In addition, it is recommended that single spacing be used within, and a double space left between, sources. Double spacing within sources is unnecessary.

The reference list appears immediately after the last page of the discussion and is paginated in the same sequence as the body of the thesis.

▶ Appendices

You should have prepared the appendices that you think are needed as part of the process of writing each part of your thesis. All that you should need to do now, therefore, is to prepare any additional appendices that are required by the department in which you are studying. When you have done this, your appendices section should be virtually complete. However, you will have to check your appendices to ensure that they comply with the necessary editorial style requirements.

Some material included as an appendix in a thesis may not comply with the necessary editorial style requirements. For instance, you might include a copy of some instrument or a questionnaire that you used in your research, or you might be required to include a printout of statistical calculations. It remains, however, that any such material must have a professional appearance.

Appendices are headed with the word "Appendix" and an upper-case letter (A, B, C, and so on) in the order to which they are first referred in the text. An exception to this is that when there is only one appendix, the alphabetical character is not necessary and so is omitted. The appendix heading is centred at the top of the page, and is typed in normal characters. The title of the appendix is centred below the heading, but is typed in italics using upper-case and lower-case letters.

Often there is no need to refer in the text to appendices required by the department. In this case, the appendices involved may be added at the end of the appendix section, and the sequence of labelling them is a matter of judgement.

Figures and tables may be presented as appendices. If more than a single figure or table is included in an appendix, they are numbered using the appendix labelling character and a number, as in, for example, "Figure A1" or "Table C2".

If an appendix is in a form such that a heading cannot be typed on it (e.g., a questionnaire or a computer print out), the heading can be typed and printed on a separate page, and cut and pasted onto the appendix, which can then be photocopied.

Appendices may be presented in landscape orientation, in which case it is headed in the same orientation.

Pagination

The appendix section of a thesis appears immediately after the reference list. Appendices, therefore, are paginated in sequence following from the last page number of the reference list. If an appendix includes more than one page, each page is separately paginated. Appendices that are presented in landscape orientation are paginated in portrait orientation.

In the event that any of the appendices are photocopies, or other material such as photographs, you will not be able to incorporate these into your computer file. If necessary, you will have to use a "forced page break" to create blank pages to allow for insertion of the required appendix.

▶ The composite file

When you have finalized the reference list and the appendices section, you can now add these two files to the file of the body of the thesis that you have already created. This will result in a file that includes the body of your thesis together with the reference list and appendices. Where necessary, this file will include blank pages to allow for insertion of figures or tables in the body of the thesis, and to allow for the insertion of any appendices that cannot be added to the file.

▶ Inserting pages

You should now print a copy of the file that incorporates the body of your thesis together with the reference list and appendices. You must check this printed copy for any flaws. For example, you might find that you have an "orphan" heading at the bottom of a page with no following text, or some similar problem. It is also possible that, if you have not been careful, you will find that you have inserted a forced page break at an inappropriate point, and so you have unwanted space at the bottom of a page. Any such flaws must be corrected. This might involve altering pagination on figures, tables, or appendices.

If you find it necessary to correct any flaws in the printed copy of your file, you will have to print a new copy after correcting them.

When you have a printed copy of the file that has no flaws in it, you should replace any pages (e.g., the first page of the introduction or a chapter) that need to be, so that they are correctly paginated. Then, you should insert any figures or tables as necessary by replacing any blank pages that you have created with the appropriate figures or tables. Finally, you should add any necessary appendices that are not included in the file.

▶ Proofreading

When you have replaced and added any necessary pages, you will have a "hard" copy of the body of your thesis, including any figures or tables involved, and the references and appendices sections. Your task now is to proofread this copy.

You will already have edited the parts of your thesis as you wrote them, and so you should not now find any problems with regard to content, continuity, grammar, spelling, punctuation, polish, or editorial style. On the other hand, you might detect a typing error such as in a figure or table number. If you detect any such problems, you will have to rectify them. Do not correct errors in handwriting. You will have to retype and print the relevant page. When doing this, make sure that you do not alter the pagination.

▶ **Preliminary pages**

Having completed the body of your thesis, and the references and appendices sections, it remains only to prepare the preliminary pages. These pages appear at the beginning of the thesis, before the first page of the introduction.

Before you begin to work on the preliminary pages, you must check any requirements given to you. However, there can be only little variation in what is required or the sequence involved. Typically, the preliminary pages will comprise

Title page
Certificate
Acknowledgements
Table of contents
List of figures
List of tables
Abstract

Title page

There is some flexibility in the layout of a title page, but it should usually be of the form illustrated in Appendix B.

The title is centred on the page. It is typed in bold, using upper-case letters for major words and those in excess of four characters.

The student's name, the department, and the name of the university are typed below the title. These are centred, but are not typed in bold. If the student already has a degree, the appropriate abbreviation may follow his or her name in the normal manner.

Wording of the statement shown on the title page will vary between universities. In general, however, the content will be similar to the example given in Appendix B. This statement is left justified.

The date of submission, in the form of month and year, is included at the bottom of the page.

Spacing on the title page is not critical, but it should be balanced to give a pleasing appearance.

The typeface used on the title page is the same as used in the text of the thesis.

The title page is not to be enclosed in a "box".

Certificate

A student submitting a thesis is required to certify that the work presented has not been submitted to any other university or for the award of any other degree, and that the content of the thesis is the student's own work. How this certificate is worded can be expected to vary between universities, but the example given in Appendix C is typical.

A point to note is that this certificate is a legally binding instrument. In particular, it certifies that no part of the content of the thesis is plagiarized, or involves any similar form of academic impropriety or dishonesty – and, except where otherwise acknowledged, is the student's own work.

Acknowledgements

The heading "Acknowledgements" is centred and typed in bold. The acknowledgement is typed in one or more paragraphs in the normal manner, and is left justified. An example of the format of an acknowledgements page is given in Appendix D.

The content of the acknowledgement page is at the student's discretion. However, any assistance of any form given to a student in the course of his or her work on the research and thesis must be acknowledged.

Table of contents

The table of contents lists the contents of the thesis in the same way, as does the table of contents in a book. This is important in a thesis because there is no index. Consequently, the only way in which material can be located with relative ease is to use the table of contents as an index.

Headings and sub-headings used in the thesis, together with the relevant page numbers, are included in the table of contents. There is usually no need to include lower level headings. It should also include the page number for the first page of the reference list, and the page (or, if there are multiple pages in an appendix, first page) number of each appendix.

An example of a table of contents is provided in Appendix E. This example illustrates the format of the table of contents for a thesis that involves more than one experiment, and that is organized into chapters (i.e., in book format). Theses written by students are often not as complex, and/or not presented in book format – in which case they will not be organized into chapters. In such a thesis, the table of contents will be a simplified version of the example given – obviously with no reference to chapters.

List of figures

A list of figures, again obviously, is a list of all figures included in the thesis together with the relevant page numbers. In this context, a figure is used to describe any form of illustration such as a graph, map, or photograph. An example of the format of a list of figures is given in Appendix F.

List of tables

A list of tables is, obviously, a list of all tables included in the thesis, together with the relevant page numbers. An example of the format of a list of tables is given in Appendix G.

List of appendices

A list of appendices is usually not included in the preliminary pages. If one is, it is simply a list of all of the appendices included in the thesis in the same format as for a list of figures or tables.

Abstract

The abstract is typed in normal fashion under the centred heading "Abstract" which is typed in bold, using upper- and lower-case letters. In a thesis, the abstract may include more than one paragraph. When this is so, the first line of each paragraph (but not the first) is indented in the normal manner. An example of the format of an abstract page is given in Appendix H.

▶ Spacing from top and bottom margins

For the Certificate, Abstract, and Acknowledgements pages, spacing from the top of the page is not critical. Rather, the text should be positioned on the page to give a pleasing appearance. Usually, this will result in the text beginning somewhat down the page, and finishing well above the bottom of the page.

▶ Pagination

Preliminary pages, with the exception of the title page, are paginated using lower-case Roman numerals centred at the bottom of the page. The first page to be paginated, therefore, will usually be the Certificate page, which will be page ii.

▶ Final proofreading

When you have completed the preliminary pages of your thesis, you will need to proofread them. In particular, look for any errors in typing or flaws in presentation, and check the pagination. When you have done this, and have corrected any errors or flaws that you detected, you need only print your preliminary pages and incorporate these into your thesis.

▶ Binding

Universities vary in their requirements with regard to the binding of theses. Traditionally, a thesis was required to be bound with a hard cover, which necessitated professional binding. However, some universities now allow for binding using one of the proprietary methods available, such as punching holes in the edge of the paper and using a plastic binding device that holds the pages in the form of a book. Some universities allow for such a form of binding for copies of the thesis that are used for examination, but require a professionally bound copy with a hard cover for the university library, and possibly another for the department library.

While proprietary binding methods do save the cost of professional binding, there is no comparison in quality. Clearly, a thesis that is professionally bound with a hard cover is more sturdy, and presents a much more professional appearance. While propriety binding is quite satisfactory for copies that are to be used for examination purposes, a student who has pride in the finished product will choose professional binding, regardless of the university requirements – at least for those copies intended for library use, and no doubt one as a personal item.

In any event, copies of theses must be permanently bound. Methods of temporary "binding", for example using spring clips, are not acceptable.

▶ Copies

The number of copies of a thesis that are required to be submitted will vary. Typically, however, one copy is required for each examiner (which usually is not returned), and one copy each for the university and department libraries. A copy is usually given to the student's supervisor as a courtesy. If an outside organization is involved in the research, in some instances a copy is given to that organization – usually as a courtesy. Finally, the student will want a personal copy. The total number of copies needed, therefore, is likely to be six or seven.

Some universities might require that an electronic copy of a thesis be lodged in addition to printed copies. When this is so, detailed requirements will be given to students.

▶ The end

After you have submitted the required number of copies of your freshly bound thesis, you can relax and celebrate a little. No doubt, you will have coursework to finish and examinations still to face, but you can at least forget about your thesis. Before you do, however, you can pause to reflect on what you have achieved. Devising and carrying out a piece of research and writing a thesis is no small feat. You will have devoted a lot of time and energy to the task. Apart from a feeling of satisfaction, you will have accomplished much that will stand you in good stead in the future.

Appendix A
Recommended style requirements for theses

(Incorporating recommended options in, and deviations from, the APA Publication Manual)

1. The typeface used throughout a thesis should be 12-point Times New Roman, with the exception that headings and labels in tables and figures may be in a sans serif typeface such as Arial.
2. Headings and major subheadings should be typed in boldface (e.g., **Method** or ***Participants***).
3. Words to be italicized are typed in italics, and not underlined.
4. A double space is left following the end of a sentence.
5. Text should not be right justified.
6. Double spacing should be used throughout the text with the exception that single spacing should be used

   - within references in a reference list, and for
   - table titles and headings
   - figure captions and labels
   - long quotations, and
   - footnotes.

7. Additional space is not left between paragraphs (i.e., double spacing is maintained throughout the text).
8. The first line of each paragraph is indented by seven spaces, with the exception of the first sentence immediately following a heading or sub-heading.
9. Quadruple spacing (i.e., double double-spacing) should be used before any heading – but not sub-heading – and before and after any figure or table included in a page of text.
10. Paper used should be standard A4 ($210 \times 297\,$mm).
11. Margins at the top and bottom, and on the right-hand side of pages should be about 35 mm. The margin on the left-hand side should be about 45 mm to allow for binding.
12. All pages, other than preliminary pages, should be paginated at the top right-hand corner, within the 35 mm top margin. If pagination cannot be readily included (e.g., on a photograph),

pages on which figures or tables are presented separately may be not paginated. However, they are numbered in that they occupy a particular page in the thesis.

13. If the thesis is in book format, the first page of each chapter is numbered at the bottom centre of the page, or not paginated.

14. Appendices are paginated as for other pages in the text and in the same sequence. If an appendix comprises multiple pages, each page is separately paginated.

15. Preliminary pages (with the exception of the title page) are paginated at the bottom centre of the page in lower case Roman numerals.

16. Figures and small tables occupying no more than half a page may be presented on a page together with text, but text may not "flow around" a figure.

17. Large figures and tables are presented on separate pages, as soon as is convenient following the first reference to the figure or table in the text. If necessary, they may be printed in landscape format.

18. A running head is not required.

Appendix B
An example of a title page

Reaction Time as a Measure of Information Processing Speed

Ian A. Hurrie, BA

Department of Psychology

University of Marble Bar

A thesis submitted in partial fulfilment of the requirements for the degree of Bachelor of Psychology with Honours.

October 2010

Appendix C
An example of a certificate page

Certificate

I certify that, to the best of my knowledge and belief, this thesis contains no material previously written or published by another person, except where due reference is made in the text. In addition, I certify that the content of this thesis represents my own unaided work, except where otherwise acknowledged.

I.N.A. Hurrie   *20 October 2010*

ii

Appendix D
An example of an acknowledgements page

Acknowledgements

I owe a debt of gratitude to my supervisor, Dr T.R. Iffic, who suggested this research project to me, and who guided me through my research and the writing of my thesis. I would also like to acknowledge the help of Dr S. Tats, who gave me useful advice and guidance in matters of analysis. In addition, I would like to thank those who gave so freely of their time to participate in my research.

Last, but not least, I would like to express my heart-felt thanks to my wife Notina, who proofread my thesis, detected flaws, and offered helpful advice. She was patient with my, at times, incoherent mumbling, hair puling, and occasional screams of frustration.

iii

Appendix E
An example of a table of contents page

Table of contents

		Page
Acknowledgements		iii
Abstract		iv
Chapter		
1	Introduction	1
	Information processing	2
	Reaction time	4
	Speed of information processing	6
2	Research approaches	9
	Common approaches	12
	Potential flaws	15
	An alternative approach	18
3	Pilot study	20
	Method	21
	Results	22
	Discussion	23
4	Experiment 1	25
	Method	26
	Results	27
	Discussion	28
5	Experiment 2	29
	Method	31
	Results	32
	Discussion	33
6	General discussion	36
	Research outcome	38
	Implications	40
	Future directions	42
References		44
Appendices		
A	Analysis of variance – Experiment 1	50
B	Analysis of variance – Experiment 2	51

iv

Appendix F
An example of a list of figures page

List of figures

Figure		Page
1	Layout of apparatus in Pilot Study	22
2	Diagrammatic illustration of the experimental task used in the Pilot Study	23
3	Layout of apparatus used in Experiment 1	26
4	Diagrammatic illustration of the experimental task used in Experiment 1	27
5	Mean reaction time scores in Experiment 1	28
6	Diagrammatic illustration of the experimental task used in Experiment 2	31
7	Mean reaction time scores in Experiment 2	32

v

Appendix G
An example of a list of tables page

List of tables

Table		Page
1	Mean reaction time scores in the Pilot Study	22
2	Details of participants in Experiment 1	26
3	Details of participants in Experiment 2	31

vi

Appendix H
An example of an abstract page

Abstract

Early studies, such as those of Donders (1869/1969) lead to the idea that the processing of information requires time, and that this results in delayed responding to stimuli. Later work, such as that of Sternberg (1969), questioned Donders' reasoning, but added to the basic concept. In particular, Sternberg showed that by manipulating the load on a processing stage the functioning of that stage could be investigated.

Extending Sternberg's work further, ...

vii

172

Notes

▶ 1 Overview

1. The masters programmes referred to here (e.g., MPsych) should be distinguished from those that can be completed by research alone.
2. A professional doctorate (e.g., DPsych) is not a PhD. While some PhD programmes in the United States of America include coursework, this is typically not the case in countries such as Australia and the United Kingdom.
3. The term "dissertation" is sometimes used in lieu of "thesis".
4. Regardless of the form in which the research is reported, in this book it is referred to as a thesis.
5. In some universities, the term "school" is used in lieu of "department".
6. Sometimes, a research problem might be suggested to a student by a prospective supervisor, and in some instances – particularly if a student is allocated to a supervisor – a research problem might be given.
7. Sometimes, this is referred to as a "project proposal".

▶ 7 A Research Proposal

1. Sometimes, this is referred to as a "project proposal".
2. At undergraduate level, research reports are sometimes referred to as practical or laboratory reports.
3. It is, of course, possible for a research project that involves pilot or validation research to include multiple experiments or studies, but for simplicity this example is based upon there being only a single experiment or study.
4. It is, of course, possible for a research project that involves multiple experiments or studies to also include pilot or validation research, but for simplicity this example is based upon there being no pilot or validation research involved.

▶ 9 The Structure and Format of a Thesis

1. At undergraduate level, research reports are sometimes referred to as laboratory or practical reports.

▶ **10   Writing a Thesis**

1. Sometimes, for various unavoidable reasons, the research carried out by students is unsuccessful and so a solution or partial solution to the research problem addressed cannot be proposed. When this is so, the thesis should show how the research involved has contributed to the future possibility of finding one.
2. In a thesis, the abstract is sometimes referred to as a "summary".

Index

abstract, 130–1, 161, 172
acknowledgements, 160, 168
advice, taking, 31–3
aim of research, 121
alternative explanation of outcome, 126, 138
analysis *see* data
analysis of data, purpose of, 123
animal subjects, 35
apparatus, 36–7, 57
appendices
  heading of, 156
  list of, 161
  pagination of, 157
  preparation of, 16–17
  use of, 117–18
applied problems and theory, 26
area of research, choice of, 23–5, 40
audio recording, 73–4

backups
  data, 52
  drafts, 131
binding, 17, 20, 162

certificate, 160, 167
changes to research design, 59, 68
chapters in a thesis, 108–10
children, 72
commitment
  time, 9, 18
  to group project, 22
computer print outs, 118
confidential material, 35
confidentiality *see* ethics
consent
  of children, 72
  form, 71–2
  of infants, 72
  informed, 69
  of parents or guardians, 72

for recording, 73–4
of school, 72
and special groups, 73
consistency, 123, 127, 139–40
contribution of the research component, 2–3
copies of thesis, 163

data
  analysis of, 5, 25, 27, 31, 49, 52, 62, 86–7, 97, 123, 136
  collection of, 4–5, 57–8, 63–4, 86–7
  group, 5, 63–4
  recording of, 51–2
  in research proposal, 86–7, 97
  see also research design
deadlines, 10, 11, 28–9
  see also target dates
debriefing, 75–6
deception *see* ethics
design of research *see* research
discussion, 126–7
drafts
  changes to, 140
  comments on, 145–7
  of discussion, 137–8
  editing of, 134–5
  figures in, 16–17
  first working, 133–4
  headings and pagination in, 134
  of introduction, 119, 135–6
  number of, 119, 144
  of parts of thesis, 145
  quality of, 143–4
  of research part of thesis, 136–7
  of research proposal, 89
  revision of first, 147
  second opinion of, 139
  submission of, 144–5
  supervisors, 142–7
  tables in, 16–17
  time for writing, 16

editing for
  consistency, 139–40
  content, 135
  detail, 140–1
editing of
  the discussion, 137–9
  the first drafts, 134–5
  the introduction, 135–6
  levels of, 134
  research part of thesis, 136
editorial style, 142, 149–50, 164–5
ethical approval, requirements for,
    69–71
ethics
  approval, 60, 63, 67–71
  basic requirements, 69–70
  and changes to research design,
    68
  children, 72
  committees, 15, 36, 55, 60,
    67, 68
  confidentiality, 69, 74–5, 77–8
  consent, 71, 77
  considerations of, 68–9
  debriefing, 75–6
  deception, 75
  explanation to participants, 70–1
  individuals who cannot give
    informed consent, 73
  infants, 72–3
  information letter, 70–1, 76
  and informed consent, 69
  medical procedures, 69
  minority groups, 69
  moral obligation, 67
  photographic or audio recordings,
    73–4
  qualitative research, 78
  and research design, 36, 51
  schools, 72
  special groups, 73
  survey research, 76–8
  time needed to gain approval, 15,
    56
examination of thesis, 112–13
expect outcome, 114
expectations of research
    component, 3–4
expected outcome in
  qualitative research, 121–2
  research proposal seminar, 97
  research proposal, 87–8, 91

external organizations
  approval, 55, 56, 60, 68
  and changes to research design,
    56
  ethics approval by, 38, 55, 56, 60,
    67–71
  involvement of, 35–6, 55
external supervision *see* supervision

feasibility of research, 33, 46–7
figures
  in a thesis, 117
  in appendices, 157
  checking, 153
  editorial style for, 153
  inserting, 155, 158
  list of, 161, 170
  numbering of, 154
  orientation of, 154–5
  pagination of, 155
  in research proposal, 88
format of a thesis, 108–9
funding of research, 38
future directions for research, 125,
    126

goals of scientific research, 26–7
group research
  choosing between projects, 40
  commitment to, 22, 64
  data analysis in, 62
  data collection in, 5, 63–4
  design of, 5
  ethics approval for, 63
  individual differences in, 5,
    6, 24
  meetings, 64–5
  obtain ethics approval for, 48
  and planning the research, 62
  problems, 65–6
  progress in, 65
  projects, 4–5, 22, 24, 29, 40, 61–2
  required, 24
  requirements of, 61–2
  research design for, 61–2
  and research problem, 24
  research proposal for, 63
  and research question, 24
  supervision of *see* supervision
  and target dates, 62, 64
  task allocations in, 62
  time plan for, 64

versus individual, 22–4
withdrawal from, 65

headings
of appendices, 156–7
in book format, 153
in discussion, 127
in drafts, 134
format of, 151, 164
in introduction, 121
levels of, 151–3
hypothesis
and data analysis, 86
development of, 52–3, 84, 93, 97,
    135–6
and expected outcome of
    research, 87–8
in group research, 5
in introduction, 93, 120
multiple, 120, 124, 128–9, 136–7
number of, 53
outcome of testing, 126, 137
in qualitative research, 27, 55, 84,
    85, 86, 97, 121–2, 127
research (or experimental), 53–4
and research design, 85
in research part of thesis, 124,
    129, 137
in research proposal, 84, 97
sequence of, 128, 136–7
testing of, 5, 52, 86, 123, 124
theoretical, 52, 126
in validation research, 32, 50–1,
    89–91, 105–8, 124, 138, 145
wording of, 53–4, 84, 123, 127–8,
    136

ideas
editing for, 138
in a research proposal, 83–4
sequence of, 133–4, 135, 137
in a thesis, 112, 113, 114–15
individual research projects, 4,
    122–3
information in a thesis, 113–14, 122,
    127, 133
information letter see ethics
informed consent see ethics
inserting pages, 158
insurance, 38
introduction
editing working drafts of, 135–6

structure of, 120, 126–7
to pilot research, 91
to research proper, 91
to thesis, 118–22
to validation research, 91
writing, 118–19, 136
see also length of, literature review
italics, 164

justification, 164

laboratory space, 60–1
legislation, 37
length of
parts of a thesis, 115–16
a research proposal, 6, 81
a thesis, 6
literature review, 6, 41–2, 111,
    118–19
literature search, 15

margins, 150, 164
materials, 36–7, 57
minority groups see ethics
monitoring work, 18
see also time
multiple experiments or studies in
    discussion, 129
and hypotheses, 93, 129
introduction, 120
in a research proposal, 91–3
in a thesis, 106–8, 124–5, 137

originality of research, 24–5, 112
outcome of testing hypotheses,
    126

pagination of
appendices, 157, 165
drafts, 134
figures, 165
main body, 155–7, 164–5
preliminary pages, 155–7, 162,
    165
tables, 165
participants
anonymity of, 69
availability of, 33–5, 61
children as, 72
debriefing of, 75–6
explanation to, 70, 71, 72
informed consent of, 69

participants – *continued*
  number needed, 34, 56–7
  in qualitative research, 34, 57
  and special groups, 35
  in survey research, 34
  voluntary participation of, 69, 70
photographic recording, 73–4
pilot research
  advisability of, 50
  changes resulting from, 50
  in discussion, 138
  drafts of, 145
  introduction to, 91
  purpose of, 50
  in research proposal, 89, 105
  in thesis, 105, 124
preliminary pages, 159–62
preliminary testing, 2, 8, 56
problem solving, 30–1, 65–6
  see also advice, taking
programmes of study, 1, 2, 8, 20, 59,
    80, 95, 111
  see also research component
proof reading, 147, 158, 162

qualitative research
  and data analysis, 52, 86, 127
  data collection in, 57–8
  in discussion, 129–30
  ethics in, 78–9
  hypotheses in, 55, 86, 97
  introduction in, 121–2
  participants in, 34
  and planning discussion, 129–30
  and planning research part of
    thesis, 125
  potential problems in, 78–9
  in research part of thesis, 125
  research proposal for, 82–3
  research question in, 52
  and structure of thesis, 104–5
  and theory, 26
  versus quantitative, 25–6

reference list, 156
requirements
  of programmes of study, 59
  of a thesis, 111–12
research
  aim of, 121
  area of, 40
  see also supervision

dangerous, 33
deception in, 75
design and data analysis, 49–61
detailed design of, 48
difficult, 32
directions for future, 126
documenting, 5–7, 27–8
expected outcome of, 61, 87–8
feasibility of, 33–8, 46–7
funding of, 38
goals of, 26–7, 88, 112
group, 5, 61–2
multiple experiments or studies in,
    61, 91–3
originality of, 24–5
outcome of, 27–8, 138
outline design of, 45–6
part of thesis, 122–5
pilot, 50
planning tasks, 62
resources needed for, 46
scope of, 4
theoretical basis of, 26, 112
time needed for, 46
validation, 50–1
weaknesses possible in, 127
research component
  contribution of, 2–3
  duration of, 2–3, 9, 11
  examination of, 111, 112–13
  expectations of, 3–4
  and group research projects, 24
  purpose of, 1, 21–2
  requirements of, 20
  scope of research in, 4
  time required for, 8–10
  two-part, 6–7, 8
research design
  changes to, 50, 59
  and data analysis, 49
  ethics in, 51, 60
  in group research projects, 61–2
  in individual research projects, 4,
    22–3, 28–9
  outline of, 45–6
  purpose of, 49–50, 52
  and research problem, 49–50
  in research proposal, 84–6, 97
  submitting to supervisor, 58
  tasks involved in, 48
  see also ethics
research part of a thesis, 122–5

research problem
  defining, 44–5, 97, 135
  finding, 43–4
  in group project, 24
  identifying, 23, 42
  importance of, 5, 42–3,
    111, 112
  in individual research projects, 4
  originality of, 24–5
  in research proposal, 84, 97
  and scientific approach, 26
  solution to, 26, 49, 97, 111–12,
    114, 125, 126
  and thesis, 111–12
research projects
  and expertise, 23–4
  group, 4–5, 22, 24, 29, 40, 61–2
  individual, 4, 22–3
  initial preparation for, 39
  quantitative *vs* qualitative, 25–6
  two-part, 111
research proposal
  content of, 81, 97
  data analysis in, 86–7
  drafts of, 89
  expected outcome in, 87–8, 91
  figures and tables in, 88
  format of, 82–3
  for group research, 63
  introduction in, 83–5, 90–1, 93
  length of, 81, 96–7
  multiple experiments or studies in,
    91–2
  pilot or validation research in,
    89–90
  planning and writing of, 83–94
  purpose of, 58–9, 80
  requirement for, 59, 80
  research design in, 85–6, 97
  structure of, 81–3, 89–90
    and multiple experiments or
      studies, 91–3
    in qualitative research, 82–3
    in quantitative research, 81–2
  submitting to supervisor, 58–9
  time plan in, 80–1
  time required for preparing, 59
  in two-part research component,
    6, 9, 80
  and use of visual aids, 98–9
  see also research component,
    two-part

research proposal seminar
  and anxiety, 95–6, 100
  audience at, 96
  content of, 96–7
  preparation of, 97–100
  presentation of, 100–1
  purpose of, 95
  reading, 98
  rehearsal of, 99–100
  requirement for, 59, 95, 111–12
  time allowed for, 99
  use of visual aids in, 98–9
research question
  answer to, 45, 49, 53, 80, 85, 86,
    97, 125, 126
  and data analysis, 86–7
  defining, 24, 45, 97
  in discussion, 138
  in group research projects,
    4–5, 24
  in individual research projects, 4
  in qualitative research, 52, 85–6
  and research design, 49–50
  in research proposal, 84
  and thesis, 112
respondents *see* participants
responsibility for
  gaining ethics approval, 60, 63
  research project, 28–9, 32
  thesis, 28–9, 32, 146, 147
running head, 150, 165

scientific goals *see* goals of scientific
  research
skills and abilities, 1, 21–2
solution to the research problem, 5,
  26, 27, 49, 53, 80, 84, 88, 94, 97,
  112, 114, 121–2, 125–6, 129–30,
  138
spacing
  in preliminary pages, 162
  of text, 151, 164
statistics in
  hypothesis testing, 123
  research proposal, 87
  see also data
structure of
  discussion, 126–7
  introduction, 120
  research part of thesis, 122
  thesis, 103–8
subjects *see* participants

supervision
  and advice, 28–9
  arranging, 22–4, 40–1
  expectations of, 28
  external, 28
  of group research projects, 29
  in group research, 29
  of individual research projects,
      28–9
  joint, 28
  maximizing the benefit of, 29
  and personality, 29–30
supervisor's role, 28
survey research
  confidentiality in, 77–8
  consent in, 77
  ethics in, 76
  information letter in, 76
  and respondents' consent, 77
  time needed for data collection in,
      57–8

table of contents, 160–1, 169
tables
  in appendices, 157
  checking of, 153
  editorial style for, 153
  inserting, 155, 158
  list of, 161, 171
  numbering of, 154
  orientation of, 154–5
  pagination of, 155, 158
  placement of, 154
  preparation of, 153–4
  in a research proposal, 88
  use of, 117
target dates, 11, 12, 13–14, 62, 64
testing, preliminary, 56
tests, 36
theoretical
  basis of research, 26
  hypothesis, 52–4, 84, 97, 120, 126,
      138
theory, in a thesis, 112, 138
thesis
  abstract in, 130–1
  aim of the research in, 121
  appendices in, 117–18
  chapters in, 109–10
  consistency in, 123, 127–8
  copies of, 163
  discussion in, 125–30

documenting the research, 5
examination of a, 111, 112–13
figures in a, 117
format of, 108–9
in group research projects, 5–6
headings in a, 121
ideas in, 114–15
information in, 113–14
introduction in, 118–22
length of, 6, 115–16
multiple experiments or studies in,
    91–3, 106–8, 115, 120, 124–5,
    129
parts of a, 115–16
pilot or validation research in,
    105–6, 124
planning of, 116–18
requirements of, 111–12
research part in, 122–5
structure of, 103–8, 110
tables in a, 117
theory in a, 112, 138
writing of a, 111
time
  allowed for research proposal
      seminar, 99
  for approval from external
      organization, 56
  estimating time needed, 12–18
  frame, 9
  for literature search, 15
  management, 10
  monitoring, 18
  needed for data collection, 57–8
  needed for research component,
      8–9
  needed for writing, 16, 119, 122,
      126
  plan, example of, 11
  plan in research proposal, 80–1
  planning, 10–12, 64
  proportions of work, 115–16
  for research, 16
  in survey research, 16
  for thinking, 17–18
title page, 159, 166
typeface, 164

validation research
  advisability of, 32
  drafts of, 145
  introduction to, 91

purpose of, 50–1
in research proposal, 89, 91
in a research proposal seminar, 91
in thesis, 105, 124
variables
in research design, 50
in research proposal, 85
variations in programmes of study, 2
visual aids, 98–9
volume of work, 21

weaknesses, 10, 130, 138, 140, 146,
147
possible in research, 126

work, volume of, 21
writing
backup of, 131
the discussion, 125–30
the introduction in parts, 136
quality of, 113
the research parts, 136–7
a research proposal, 83, 84, 86,
87, 88
some advice on, 132
target dates for, 14
of thesis, 111
the thesis, in parts, 16
see also drafts